THE
POWER *of*
PERSISTENT
PRAYER

Books by
Cindy Jacobs

The Power of Persistent Prayer

Possessing the Gates of the Enemy

The Reformation Manifesto

CINDY JACOBS

THE
POWER
of
PERSISTENT
PRAYER

PRAYING *with* GREATER
PURPOSE *and* PASSION

BETHANYHOUSE
MINNEAPOLIS, MINNESOTA

Published by Bethany House Publishers
11400 Hampshire Avenue South
Bloomington, Minnesota 55438

Bethany House Publishers is a division of
Baker Publishing Group, Grand Rapids, Michigan.

Printed in the United States of America

In keeping with biblical principles of creation stewardship, Baker Publishing Group advocates the responsible use of our natural resources. As a member of the Green Press Initiative, our company uses recycled paper when possible. The text paper of this book is comprised of 30% post-consumer waste.

green press INITIATIVE

Library of Congress Cataloging-in-Publication Data

Jacobs, Cindy.
    The power of persistent prayer : praying with greater purpose and passion / Cindy Jacobs.
        p. cm.
    Summary: "A concise and practical guide to an effective prayer life. It includes basics like 'Why pray?' and 'How do I pray?' followed by more complex topics such as fasting and spiritual warfare as they relate to prayer"—Provided by publisher.
    Includes bibliographical references (p.   ).
    ISBN 978-0-7642-0503-3 (hardcover : alk. paper) 1. Prayer—Christianity. I. Title.
    BV210.3.J33   2010
    248.3′2—dc22

                                                             2010015680

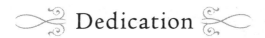 # Dedication

This book is lovingly dedicated to:

Lilli Janina Jacobs

(my first granddaughter)

About the Author

CINDY JACOBS is one of the most visible leaders in the modern prayer movement, calling for intercession, repentance, and renewal worldwide. She and her husband, Mike, are the founders of Generals International, working to achieve social transformation through intercession and prophetic ministry. Cindy has written several bestselling books, including *Possessing the Gates of the Enemy* and *The Voice of God*. Her television program, *God Knows,* is seen in the U.S. on the God Channel as well as around the world. She travels and speaks internationally to groups of hundreds of thousands each year in churches and conference centers. Cindy and Mike are the parents of two grown children and reside in Dallas, Texas.

Contents

Introduction

As I have traveled around the world leading prayer gatherings and initiatives, it is not unusual for someone to pull me aside and whisper, "Cindy, how can I *really* see my prayers answered? Can you tell me the secrets that God has shown you through your years as a prayer leader?"

Often as I am asked that question, my mind will flash back over my years of leading others in prayer. As you will read in the pages of this book, I didn't start out with the aspiration of becoming a general of intercession, believe me. I sincerely wanted to be a stay-at-home mom, but God had other plans. I was not, at first, a willing officer of prayer! You see, my husband, Mike, and I did not set out to claim the title *generals of intercession*. Frankly, it is the name that came to be given to our ministry over the years—not so much by us at first, but rather by being introduced over and over as prayer generals.

Finally, through the nudging of friends like Kyle Duncan, who edited this book, I have written down these "secrets of a prayer general" for all to read. I have chosen the topics for you in a careful fashion so you would have the keys needed to see your prayers answered.

These keys to answered prayer are gleaned from my times of prayer in places like Iraq, where we stood on rocky mountainsides praying for wars to shift. Such dramatic scenes were contrasted by quiet moments of anguish in my prayer closet, bent over on my knees, weeping for my own generations (mine and my family members').

I would like to take a journey with you in this book. Sit down with it in your morning devotional time and teach it to your prayer groups. We will begin with the most basic but sometimes unasked question: "Why do we need to pray at all? Since a loving and everywhere-present God knows our needs, why do we need to ask in prayer?"

For those of you who are more seasoned intercessors, this may seem elementary, but I assure you that we cannot afford to skip steps as we share with others how to pray. We often assume that people know many things that they do not know and thus leave huge gaps in their understanding of the purposes of God. That is why we are starting with this most foundational question: "Why pray?" Not only that, but like me, hopefully you will discover ways to deepen your own prayer life, even though you might have been a prayer leader for many decades.

While reading, I want you to imagine we are sitting down together, having a conversation over a cup of coffee or tea. I want to share my heart with you in this book in an intimate way, as well as give you a window into times when I was struggling to break through in persistent prayer.

A critical question that we will look at in our conversation is what I call *the case for persistent prayer.* Maybe you have prayed for someone until you are simply exhausted with praying that particular prayer. Don't give up! Persistent prayer works, and you will see the answer come. Many times the battle is the fiercest right before the tide turns. What do I mean by this? Just before a breakthrough, your husband gets the grouchiest or your child seems to find new and unique ways to sin and embarrass you. I wrote chapter 2, "The Case for Persistent Prayer," to give you strength and grace as you continue to battle on in your prayer times against impossible odds.

I love the chapter on fasting! (Well, mostly I do—the fruit of it, anyway.) Actually, my flesh absolutely hates to go without food (especially ice cream). Read the chapter and then find a partner as you pursue the depth of prayer with this powerful "rocket-booster" to intercession.

While looking back at the chapters I've written (I am finishing the introduction last!), I kept thinking, *Oh, that is exactly what I wanted to share with you, reader,* or *That is the best secret yet!*

Since I'm a musician myself, and I am completely sold on the use of praise in our prayers, I had to include the chapter "Persistent Praise." My friend (and by faith, future prayer general), that chapter simply is a must-read. You are going to love it!

A book on prayer would not be complete, in my opinion, without a chapter on intergenerational praying. Moms, this is going to touch your hearts! All of us—whether or not we have our own physical children—know that we need to leave a legacy and that successive generations need to pray together.

You will probably be able to tell that the very last chapter, "Kingdom Intercession," is a message that is deeply on my heart today. I want to see the nations of the earth changed through persistent prayer to see *His kingdom come; His will be done on earth as it is in heaven!*

Ready to learn the secrets and keys that I've learned from God's Word and others to get your prayers answered? Let's begin the journey. . . .

Chapter One

Why Pray?

One day in 1989, I was sitting at our dining room table in Weatherford, Texas, in the midst of writing my first book, *Possessing the Gates of the Enemy*. I had papers scattered all over the place and was deeply engrossed in thought, when I suddenly felt a small hand reach up and tug on my shirt.

"Mom, Mom," came the insistent voice of my eight-year-old son, Daniel. "I need you to come with me right now."

At this point I did what most busy moms do—I tried to stall. "Not now, Daniel, I'm working!" Grown-up projects always seem to be much weightier and more important than those of eight-year-old boys, don't they? Of course, Daniel had figured out long before that it sometimes took a bit of nudging when I was engrossed in a book or in some other "critical" motherly task such as cooking. So he did what little boys do: He ratcheted up the volume of his voice and increased the fervency of his plea.

"Mama, you must come right now!" Envisioning a crisis

such as our large calico cat treed by a dog, or all the gerbils loose and scampering for crevasses where they could hide to increase their population, I bounded out of the dining room chair. Seizing the moment, Daniel took my hand to guide me to the object of his urgent need: our mini-trampoline covered by a tablecloth (at least, that's what it looked like to me). Puzzled, I gave Daniel the this-better-be-important-son look that mothers are famous for. He then commanded me to kneel down. All of a sudden the atmosphere around that small round object changed.

I felt a holy hush come over my soul as I heard the focus of my motherly affections say to me, "Mom, this is my altar, and we need to pray!"

Out of that small boy's mouth poured a torrent of prayer. He pled with God for his friends, for our family, and other matters of concern to his heart. I was struck by the fact that such a short person could pray such a God-sized prayer! Then, as I was getting totally caught up in the splendor of the moment, he looked at me as if seeing me for the first time since he commanded me to kneel, and said, "Mom, you can leave now. I need to be alone with God."

Right then I knew that something profound had transpired. Daniel had touched God in such a way that I was, indeed, an intruder in the travail of a soul that was anything but junior-sized to his heavenly Father. Ever so quietly, I slipped away.

Later on Daniel became his typical self as I extricated him from a fight with his ten-year-old sister, Mary. I think they were quibbling over whose turn it was to choose the next highly important television program. Yet I had been forever marked by that moment, kneeling at that little altar in the presence of God and my son's intercession. Through his *insistence* that I be his prayer partner that day, Daniel taught me something about *persistence* in my own personal pursuit of God.

Why Do We Need to Pray?

While reading that story you might have been thinking, *Why would God need a little child to pray like that? Can't God fix the world without the help of a seven-year-old—or any other person, for that matter—to intercede with insistence and persistence?*

Put another way, one of the questions I am commonly asked is: "Since God has all power and authority, why do we need to pray at all? Doesn't He know what we need before we ask?" After all, Matthew 6:8 says: "Your Father knows the things you have need of before you ask Him."

This is a foundational question. For those of us who have been raised to believe in the importance of prayer, it might cause us to question the audacity of a person who would ask such a question. *Why pray? Why don't we just leave our lives in the hands of an all-knowing, all-wise Creator without our personal interaction at all?*

In fact, prayer is a beautiful, sometimes baffling interchange. If you had never heard of prayer before, what would you think if someone told you prayer entails walking around talking to someone you cannot see and expecting that person to hear you and to care? Kind of odd, huh? But not only does God hear us and care about us, He will answer us!

This divine exchange we call prayer is marvelous, and most people who engage in prayer believe that God is indeed listening. At first blush it seems mysterious, yet to those with faith it is as natural as taking a breath—yet supremely supernatural.

Have you ever felt like when you prayed there really wasn't

anyone on the other end? Perhaps you even came to the conclusion that if there is a God who is listening to you, He—for some unknown reason—doesn't care to give you an answer. If that is the case, why continue to pray at all? Read on, dear friend, and we will explore this utterly important question.

When I was a little girl, I remember a situation with a friend who did not appreciate my bossing her around. (You see, even as a child I was a little general.) I had definite ideas of what game we were to play, who would stand where when we played that game, and *always,* I was to be the leader. I'll never forget the day when my friend, tired of my taking over her life and my always being the person in charge, reared up to her full height and said to me, "Who died and made you God?" What she meant, of course, was that I should back off and let someone else have a say for a while in how our little world was run!

Of course, we are not God, nor does anyone in his right mind want to have His job! God has ordained His world to function through believing prayer, and He has chosen us to partner with Him in the divine interaction called prayer.

As His children, we are His divinely chosen stewards of the earth. Prayer—walking and talking with our Father—is integral to the Christian life because it brings us back to the reason we were created in the first place. He wants to take us back to our created mandate—all the way back to the garden.

I love gardens, and Eden must have been a spectacular place. Eden was the first command center for earth. It was from that place of beauty and relationship that Adam and Eve were to fulfill their commission to "be fruitful and multiply; fill the earth and subdue it; have dominion over the fish of the sea, over the birds of the air, and over every living thing that moves on the earth" (Genesis 1:28).

The commentary on this passage in the *Spirit-Filled Life Bible* says: "God created man to be His kingdom agent, to rule and subdue the rest of creation, including the aggressive satanic forces, which would soon infringe upon it."[1] This brings me to this critical point: *Without walking and talking with God in prayer, we will never fulfill our original design and the earth will lack order and fruitfulness.*

God put Adam and Eve in Eden, a place of magnificent splendor, delighted them with pets and animals—from birds to boa constrictors to baboons—and let them walk and talk with Him. Now that sounds good! They sinned, however, and lost the personal face-to-face relationship with their Maker. However, God never rescinded His original mandate that we were to be His earth managers.

Prayer ushers in order out of chaos, pulls peace out of confusion and destruction, and brings joy in the midst of sorrow. It takes what Satan meant for evil and brings us good. Prayer— and the pulse that beats between us and God through it—is the essence of who we are as believers. Our life without prayer has no meaning, power, or purpose. Neither does the life of the people of the nations of the earth.

As a believer, can you conceive of one or more days in your life without a single conversation with God? Not even a "God, why did this happen to me?" or "O God, save me!" when someone cuts you off in traffic. Prayer for the Christian is as natural as taking a breath. It is a relationship that is extraordinary! We pray (or talk with God) because it is part of the DNA stamped into our genetic makeup. Quite simply, we were created to talk with God.

Our Destiny as His Bride

This still brings us to the question of why. Why does God need us to pray for His will to be done? Paul E. Billheimer suggests that our life is on-the-job training to enter into our destiny as the bride of Christ.

In his book *Destined for the Throne*, Billheimer presents a case that gives an eternal perspective to our role to help bring order to the earth through prayer and intercession. His premise is this:

> Our life on the earth is not only to deal with the here and now, but to prepare us to share the throne of the universe with her Divine Lover and Lord as a judicial equal. Therefore she must be trained, educated, and prepared for her queenly role. The Church (later on to become the Bride) must learn the art of spiritual warfare, of overcoming evil forces in preparation for her assumption of the throne following the Marriage Supper of the Lamb. To enable her to learn the technique of overcoming, God ordained the infinitely wise program of believing prayer. He did not ordain prayer primarily as a way of getting things done. It is His way of giving the Church "on the job" training in overcoming the forces hostile to God. This world is a laboratory in which those destined for the throne are learning in actual practice how to overcome Satan and his hierarchy. The prayer closet is the arena which produces the overcomer.[2]

As Billheimer points out, we see in our role as intercessors that we are not only to guard and protect the earth but also to prepare for a bright and glorious future with our heavenly bridegroom, Jesus Christ.

Have you ever wondered what Adam and Eve talked about during their times of fellowship with God in the cool of the day? I used to think they were just chatting. You know, saying things like, "Well, God, what kind of day did you have today?" And God answering, "Well, today we had a wonderful time, where all the angels worshiped me and we danced on the sea of glass." (Of course, not to say that wouldn't be absolutely glorious!)

As I have looked at the full counsel of God's words, however, there is a pattern established that I believe started in the garden. This is it: Adam and Eve were being trained by God to rule and reign and see His kingdom come and His will be done on earth as it is in heaven—while they walked and talked with God.

This is why when Jesus taught His disciples to pray, He brought His counsel around full circle and told them to pray like this: *"Father, let your kingdom come and your will be done."* Jesus walked and talked with the disciples just like God did in the beginning with Adam and Eve. It was full circle for God. It must have been absolutely wonderful for Him to have this kind of face-to-face communion again with His creation. Can you imagine it?

God loves to talk with us!

My husband, Mike, and I have two children. Perhaps some of you have children as well. Even though my children are grown, I love to talk with them. Throughout my day or between the times when we can connect, I think about what I am going to say to them. I also love to talk with my four grandchildren. I rehearse over and over in my mind what I am going to share either in person or on the phone.

For instance, the other day, Zion, who is three, said to his mom, "Mom, when you said that, you made my feelers cry." Oh my, I love that!

God enjoys the things we say to Him too! He loves us and gets tickled by the things we talk about in prayer, the songs we sing; He receives joy from the sweet things we say each day. Prayer is talking with God. It is relationship; our talking to God makes Him happy.

I also talk with my grandchildren in order to instruct them. My three grandsons tell me about the children who are bullies or the girls who chase them to kiss them on the cheek. Of course, being a wise and loving grandmother, I always say, "Someday

God is going to bring you someone who loves you, someone to give your kisses to."

Each of my grandchildren is unique and special, as are both of my children. Zion is a little general like me and his mother. He said to her the other day, "Mommy, I am the boss." She replied to him, "No, Zion, I'm the boss." After which he took both of her cheeks in his hands, gazed directly into her eyes, and compromised with, "Mommy, *we're* the boss." Oh, that sounds familiar! Zion has a gift of leadership and ruling, and one day God will use him in a special way to see His kingdom come and His will be done on earth as it is in heaven.

Malachi loves to make money, and Caden is so loving and sensitive. I walk and talk with each of them differently on a regular basis. God's relationship with us is the same: We are called to rule with Him in different areas and on different bases. The things one person will talk to God about may be slightly different than another, and there are times when all of us will pray for the needs of others together.

In addition to family, God has given me friends that I treasure and love. I am blessed with what I like to call my "heart friends." I tell them the deepest things I am feeling, pondering, or dreaming. In addition to earthly friends, God is my best heart friend. I get very, very honest with Him in our conversations.

God created the earth with the necessity for prayer built into the equation. He already had the angels and all of heaven, but He wanted fellowship with us.

Each day, God thinks about you and is excited when you wake up because He wants to see you grow, fulfill your gifts, and learn to be an intercessor who prays to change lives and situations around you. He is trusting us to pray the prayers needed to see His will accomplished on the earth: to bring hope to the hopeless, justice instead of injustice, and blessings instead of

poverty. God wants us to take care of this earth. He is also looking at His bride-to-be with longing affection, as we learn to be a
future mate worthy of Him.

That is why He has placed so many reminders in His Word
of the importance of prayer. For instance:

> I looked for someone to stand up for me against all this,
> to repair the defenses of the city, to take a stand for me and
> stand in the gap to protect this land so I wouldn't have to
> destroy it. I couldn't find anyone. Not one.
>
> EZEKIEL 22:30 *THE MESSAGE*

In his excellent book *Intercessory Prayer,* Dutch Sheets says
about this Scripture:

> The passage is clearly saying, "While My justice demanded
> judgment, My love wanted forgiveness. Had I been able to
> find a human to ask Me to spare this people, I could have. It
> would have allowed Me to show mercy. Because I found no
> one, however, I had to destroy them." I don't like the implica-
> tions of this passage any more than you do. I don't want the
> responsibility. I don't like to consider the ramifications of a
> God who has somehow limited Himself to us earthlings. But
> in light of these and other passages, as well as the condition
> of the world, I can come to no other conclusion.[3]

I have always said that the newspaper is the Christian's report
card. When you look at sections that describe the crime rate going
down, abortion clinics being closed, floods being averted, and
the rains of heaven filling dry and thirsty lakes, I always think,
"For sure, someone prayed." Prayer brings God's blessing and the
lack of it causes the earth to suffer and people to be destructive.
Evil powers rule and reign without prayer. We need to intercede

to restrain Satan and his minions from wrecking our lives and that of our nation.

As you wake up each day, open your eyes to your beloved Redeemer who wants to talk to you about your life and the day to come and to give you assignments concerning His will. He wants His will released into the earth through you. Your faithful, persistent, daily-bread prayers have the potential to change the face of the earth—believe it or not.

Simply put, God wants to accomplish His will, and He is waiting for us to ask Him what part He wants us to play. Asking is biblical. Why? Because God has told us so. You might reply, "I don't want to ask. I just want Him to give me what I need without asking." Remember how I said that my playmate from childhood made the comment "Who died and made you God?" I am not God and I don't make the rules. The point is this: God says to ask, and God is God and we are not.

When my children were growing up, they grew weary of my talking about obeying authority. Over and over I said to them, "When someone in authority over you tells you to jump, you reply, 'How high?' " In fact, I would barely start giving my "authority speech" when they would give me that certain look, and with one eyebrow raised, say, "We know, Mom, when our teacher says jump, we say, 'How high?' " I guess they did listen to me sometimes.

One of my favorite Bible passages in this regard is found in Luke 11, right after Jesus taught His disciples how to pray. This is a profound passage on persistent prayer and petition (or asking). Here is where the word *ask* is used specifically:

> Ask and you'll get;
> Seek and you'll find;
> Knock and the door will open.

Don't bargain with God. *Be direct. Ask for what you need.* This is not a cat-and-mouse, hide-and-seek game we're in. If your little boy asks for a serving of fish, do you scare him with a live snake on his plate? If your little girl asks for an egg, do you trick her with a spider? As bad as you are, you wouldn't think of such a thing—you're at least decent to your own children. And don't you think the Father who conceived you in love will give the Holy Spirit when you ask him?

LUKE 11:8–13 *THE MESSAGE*

The Beauty of Asking

Ask. What a powerful word! Strong's dictionary lists various ways the word is translated in Scripture: "beg, call for, crave, desire, require."[4]

Sometimes when I ask God for something for my family, the unction to pray is so deep that all I can do is groan, "O God, protect them. Give them wisdom." I am glad that God can translate my deepest weeping and groaning as *asking*. The Bible says in Romans 8:26:

Likewise the Spirit also helps in our weaknesses. For we do not know what we should pray for as we ought, but the Spirit Himself makes intercession for us with groanings which cannot be uttered.

I long for the destiny of my family to be fulfilled as well as that of my church, city, and nation.

Paul felt this way for his people, the Jews:

You need to know that I carry with me at all times a huge sorrow. It's an enormous pain deep within me, and I'm never free of it. I'm not exaggerating—Christ and the Holy Spirit are

my witnesses. It's the Israelites. . . . If there were any way I could
be cursed by the Messiah so they could be blessed by him, I'd
do it in a minute. They're my family. I grew up with them.
They had everything going for them—family, glory, covenants,
revelation, worship, promises, to say nothing of being the race
that produced the Messiah, the Christ, who is God over every
thing always. Oh yes!

ROMANS 9:1–5 *THE MESSAGE*

Many times I have had conversations with intercessors who
feel that deep groaning for the Jewish people today. In fact, I
entered into this type of deep, lamenting intercession for the
Jewish people during a visit to Israel a few years ago.

It happened the night before we were to leave to return to
the United States. Mike and I had packed, and as often is the
case when leaving Israel, we had only about an hour or so to
rest before leaving for the airport at two in the morning. As I
lay down, I thought about our trip and began to see the faces
of the Israeli people—some of whom I had met, others random
faces from the crowd. Then stories resonated through my mind
of the sin that is rampant in the streets of Tel Aviv—a modern
city with a thriving night-life culture.

Our hotel was near the ancient city of Joppa. We had stood
on the very site where Jonah ran from God to Tarsus rather
than face his destiny to tell Nineveh to repent. (I can relate
to Jonah's dilemma, as God has called me to pray for nations
to repent!) A short distance from that historic site stands the
cosmopolitan city of Tel Aviv, with its high-end shops, clubs,
and bars. As of this writing, there are very few Messianic believers in the city, despite the diligent work of friends like Ari and
Shira Sorko Ram.

As I was resting, the time to leave for the airport fast approach-
ing, my thoughts shifted to the lines of tour buses that hug the

ancient city roads as people from around the world flood into Israel to walk where Jesus walked. Who knows how many thousands have stood on the dusty cobblestones of old Jerusalem—perhaps tens of millions.

All of a sudden, a deep guttural cry erupted from inside of me, "O God, we have failed!" How could so many groups of Christian believers from across the globe flow through this Holy Land (literally) and yet have so little (seeming) impact on the spiritual lives of the nation and region?! By this time, tears were coursing down my cheeks. Deep within, I knew that for all our intercession for the land of Israel, the government, and the Jews worldwide, we had largely failed to reach them for the Messiah.

Perhaps I took up a small portion of Paul's intercession for his people that night. As I lay there during that early morning travail, I asked God for their souls and for more laborers to be sent into the harvest field. I have also experienced this kind of weeping and intercession while in Kuwait for the Arabic people and the Middle East. This same travail welled up in me while in Iraq. I will cover this more extensively in chapter 10, "Kingdom Intercession."

There are many "asking" Scriptures in the Bible. Here are just a few of them:

1. Ask the Lord for rain. (Zechariah 10:1)
2. Ask anything in My name. (John 14:14)
3. Ask for wisdom. (James 1:5)
4. Ask for the Holy Spirit. (Luke 11:13)

God wants us to *ask Him* to do the things that release His will into every part of creation and each part of our everyday lives. Sometimes it's the asking that is difficult as we wrestle with our own doubts, personal circumstances, or the apparent hopelessness of a situation. To ask is not always easy—but it is the essence of persistent prayer.

Many have quoted appropriately John Wesley's famous statement on the subject: *"God does nothing on the earth save in answer to believing prayer."*

I want to challenge you to pray as you read this book! Don't let Satan tell you your prayers are insignificant, don't measure up, or any other such lie. Begin asking and believing that your prayers do make a difference. Every single prayer counts!

This is what this book is about: Asking in prayer and not giving up—the power of persistent prayer. Asking and believing until you see the answers.

If at this time situations around you make it seem like prayer doesn't work or that you are weak and powerless to affect the status quo, know that it is not so! God will provide you with keys to unlock the mysterious—and at times elusive—in order to see your prayers answered.

Get ready to learn how to unlock the closed doors of unanswered prayers. The earnest, effectual prayer of a righteous believer avails much. *The Message* puts it this way:

> The prayer of a person living right with God is something powerful to be reckoned with!
>
> JAMES 5:16

Chapter Two

The Case for Persistent Prayer

$\mathcal{W}$e love to hear testimonies that are a result in part of our faithfulness in prayer, but walking through to the point of testimony can be an emotional roller coaster. Take the case of Tim and Elisa Roberts. I first heard of them during a service at Trinity Church in Cedar Hill, Texas, where Mike and I are members. For those of you given to sudden tears: You'd better grab the Kleenex now.

Tim and Elisa are a young couple, deeply in love, to whom God gave their hearts' desire through the adoption of a handsome young son, Matthew. Adoption was especially meaningful to Elisa, as she also was adopted.

Another prayer the two of them had earnestly petitioned was that God would give them a biological child. Of course they knew this would in no way diminish the miracle of their chosen son; rather, it would add another dimension to their joy. So Tim and Elisa prayed. And prayed some more. One year of intercession turned into two, then three, until it became six long years of persistent prayer—2,190 hours of waiting on God!

During that time, Hannah's prayer, found in 1 Samuel 1:11, became Elisa's anguished cry:

> Oh, God-of-the-Angel-Armies,
> If you'll take a good, hard look at my pain,
> If you'll quit neglecting me and go into action for me
> By giving me a son,
> I'll give him completely, unreservedly to you.
> I'll set him apart for a life of holy discipline.
>
> THE MESSAGE

Both Tim and Elisa decided that when God gave them another child, they would dedicate the baby to the Lord.

Finally, one day at church, a visiting evangelist prayed for Tim and said words something like this, "God is going to give you three children because He is going to give you what you most want." The evangelist went on with an odd comment, "No more dogs."

Dogs?! What does that have to do with children? Simply this: Tim had just bought Elisa another dog to try and help ease the pain of wanting another child. Thank God for dogs, but right now their heavenly Father was interested in releasing a miracle through the young couple.

At last, their prayer turned into reality in the form of one perfectly formed little girl. Anyone looking at that child could see that her name had to be Bella, for she was beautiful. Bella's triumphant entry into this world came on August 29, 2007.

Tim and Elisa's joy was beyond imagination. After six long

years, they held the answer to their prayers in their arms! Bella was perfect.

Two months of rejoicing later, little Bella was tucked into bed one night, only this time she didn't wake up on earth—instead, she made the journey to heaven. The autopsy report revealed she had died in her sleep of a viral infection. There are moments in all of our lives when we are tempted to believe that God isn't fair and that the situations in our life can be quite capricious. This would be one of those times. For Elisa and Tim, their trust in the loving Father was deeply tested during that anguished time after Bella's death.

For a while I did not hear anything else about this young couple. Of course that is not unusual—I travel so much that I wonder if my home church is going to offer me a visitor's card!

But in God's wonderful goodness, a bit more than a year later, I was in the church service one Sunday when a young couple stood before the congregation with a small child in their arms. It seemed they were going to give a testimony.

As they began to speak, I came to the startling realization that this was the same Tim and Elisa who had prayed so persistently for a child, only to have little Bella die after only two months.

They shared a bit of their journey after Bella went home to be with the Lord and how Tim had shared with Elisa, "I'd like to have a little-boy version of Bella."

At this point, the proud father looked down at his son, their third child, and I was getting a little teary-eyed. *How precious,* I thought, *God was so faithful to give them another baby.*

Hold on, because I was yet to fathom the faithfulness of God in their lives. They announced the child's name: Justice Michael Roberts.

"*Justice?* Interesting name," I mused. The testimony continued.

Tim and Elisa had gone for a routine checkup to see how the pregnancy was advancing, when the doctor commented that he felt they should go ahead and take the baby that day.

That night, November 29, 2008, at precisely 6:02 p.m., Justice made his premier into the world—exactly fifteen months to the minute from the time little Bella had been born. God had fulfilled the prayer of the evangelist that they would have three children—and they did so with chronological flourish!

Justice indeed had arrived for the Roberts family. And that's not all. Tim and Elisa have established a foundation called *Bella's Springs* in her memory, based on the passage in Psalm 84:6–7:

> As they pass through the Valley of Baca, [or weeping, as it is sometimes translated], they make it a place of springs; the autumn rains also cover it with pools. They go from strength to strength till each appears before God in Zion.
>
> NIV

They have already helped poor children in Vietnam and Zimbabwe with things such as open-heart surgery. Bella now lives through a child's beating heart in Vietnam and warm bodies in Africa from the blankets they've supplied.

Their story doesn't end there though. The morning that I called Tim and Elisa to interview them for this chapter, Tim answered and told me that they were getting ready to leave for his father's funeral. Tim's dad came to the Lord a month and a half before he passed away, after they prayed for him for eight years. They raised funds in his dad's memory for *Bella's Springs Foundation*.

I say this, *"His mercies are new every morning. Great is His faithfulness"* (see Lamentations 3:22–23). Just think: Mr. Roberts is in heaven holding his little granddaughter, Bella, and Justice now lives in his son's household. Now that is a very, very sweet thought.

Tenacious Toward God's Promises

What if Tim and Elisa had not been persistent in their prayers? They had a promise from God, but that promise was hard to obtain. This is why Jesus, the master storyteller, wove together such in-depth and descriptive stories about never losing heart when we have a request that we want God to answer. Jesus knew that His stories would leave a trail of hope for couples like Tim and Elisa—and people like us—not to grow weary or lose faith in His ability to both hear and answer our prayers.

I can only imagine how the crowd that followed Jesus must have felt as He shared the various parables He told at particular times, in fitting locations. I can picture His disciples and those gathered to hear Him, whispering among themselves while they waited for Him to begin, pondering what kind of parable the rabbi would share that day.

Because I want you to understand the richness of Jesus' effectiveness as a word crafter, we need to get a glimpse of the culture of the day. I will highlight some culturally pertinent points as we go along.

Imagine it is one of those days. The crowd has gathered. Jesus is preparing to speak. In this case, the story He chooses to tell is recorded in Luke 18:1–8. But before we relay the story, here's the punch line: We are never to give up praying and never give up hoping (or losing heart) that God will answer. This is why the story of Justice Michael Roberts is important for us: It is a modern-day example of an intercessory cry that flows beautifully with the following illustration of one woman's plea for justice in an unjust age:

> Then Jesus told his disciples a parable to show them that they should always pray and not give up. He said: "In a certain town there was a judge who neither feared God nor cared about men. And there was a widow in that town who kept coming to him with the plea, 'Grant me justice against my adversary.'
>
> "For some time he refused. But finally he said to himself, 'Even though I don't fear God or care about men, yet because this widow keeps bothering me, I will see that she gets justice, so that she won't eventually wear me out with her coming!'"
>
> And the Lord said, "Listen to what the unjust judge says. And will not God bring about justice for his chosen ones, who cry out to him day and night? Will he keep putting them off? I tell you, he will see that they get justice, and quickly. However, when the Son of Man comes, will he find faith on the earth?"
>
> LUKE 18:1–8 NIV

This portrait of the persistent widow is an illustration of a cultural worst-case scenario for that day and time in Israel. Jesus shared it to spotlight how God truly does answer impossible prayers.

First of all, the story included a judge. At that time judges would travel the country and sit in tents to pass judgment on cases. Oftentimes they were part of a corrupt system and would only take a case if they were paid a bribe. Legal and judicial corruption was a big problem in Jesus' time, just as it is in many countries of the world today. I have heard stories about a certain Latin American nation where judges turn the pages of a case about to be heard and decide the outcome dependent upon how much money is resting between its pages.

And now the second point: Women of that day did not have the same measure of legal recourse as men. They were simply not heard at all in the courtroom; there was no justice for them. So here we have the case of a poor woman with no husband (a widow) coming before a judge to plead her case.

As you consider the parable of the persistent widow, take note of how God was multitasking as Jesus relayed the story, making several points in a way that the culture could understand. For starters, He was elevating the status of women by using an illustration concerning a woman. And not just any woman, but a widow—a woman without a man in a culture where men were the key to status, authority, and one's social station. So on a deeper, related level, Jesus is showing His love for the poor and lowly, He is seizing an opportunity to shower His merciful heart and care upon the downtrodden.

This is the take-away from the passage (Luke 18:1–8):

> None of you are too poor, lonely, or without judicial recourse to receive justice in the court of heaven. God is always just, always good, and always ready to hear your prayers!

The Power of Desperation

I wonder why the woman was so persistent. I believe it was because she had nowhere else to turn. She was absolutely desperate. Perhaps that is your case as you read this chapter. For instance, are you currently in a court case and praying for justice?

In the chapter "Praying the Word," I am going to add some special prayers for you to use in intercession.

You might also be desperate to receive an answer from God on a very serious matter. Persistence is the answer.

When I get a picture in my mind of persistence, I often think of when my grandson Malachi was four years old. He was and is a single-minded child, as are my other grandchildren. (God didn't consider the word *compliant* when He knitted my grandchildren together in their mothers' wombs!) If Malachi at age four wanted me to take him to the park, he would start working on me early in his visit.

"Nonnie," he would say with that cute smile, "isn't it a good day to go to the park?" At that point I might look outside and think, *No, Malachi, it is windy and I'm tired, and I don't feel like venturing out.*

My grandkids, however, are masterful at devising plans to motivate a woman of my age to want to get out and take a walk to the park, swing the three of them, catch them going up and down the slide, and do various other forms of physical exertion.

They are persistent in their petitions for a number of reasons. One is that at their age, they cannot go to the park alone. This means they need an adult to take them (i.e., usually me). They are also very sure of their present need to receive the answer they desire.

In the case of the widow, she wanted justice from an adversary; she wanted to be avenged. The judge, *unlike* a doting grandparent, had no compassion.

The passage also describes how the woman "bothered" him, or "troubled" (NKJV) him. The word *troubled* means "to reach forth to beat another or to cause another trouble."[1] Another way to say it is that she vexed him! (I like that word too.) I really love the next part of Luke 18:5, because it says the unjust judge didn't want the woman to "weary" (NKJV) him or "wear him out." If you are like me and love to look up the meaning of words in the Greek, you will love what the word *weary* means: "to beat down, to blacken the eye."[2] The judge did not want the woman to give him a "black eye" (i.e., hurt his reputation) in the community.

I wonder how she brought him to that place? Maybe every time he went to the synagogue, she was there. Or perhaps she tagged after him as he hurried past the marketplace on Friday afternoon, prior to sundown and the beginning of the Sabbath. Or when he was trying to go into the tent for court, she nipped at his heels with her pleas. Basically he gave her justice simply to get rid of her. What a woman! In the U.S., we have a slang expression that fits her spunk: "You go, girl!"

The Mystery of God's Timing

This reminds me of the story I read about Roger Sims, a hitchhiker making his way home from military service, still wearing his army uniform. He had his suitcase in tow and was at last picked up by a man driving a new black Cadillac. The date was May 7.

The well-dressed, nice-looking man said to him when he piled into the car, "Where are you headed?" As they pulled away from the side of the road, the man introduced himself as Mr. Hanover, a fifty-something businessman from Chicago.

Roger, a Christian, kept feeling a compulsion to witness to the man. He did, and to his surprise, the man pulled over and prayed to receive Jesus Christ. He said to Roger, "This is the greatest thing that has ever happened to me."

Five years later, after marrying and having a little boy, Roger came across Mr. Hanover's business card. Since he was heading to Chicago on a trip, he decided to look up the fellow with whom he had prayed five years before.

Once in the city, he went to Hanover Enterprises and was told it was impossible to see Mr. Hanover, but that his wife was available. As she approached Roger, Mrs. Hanover seemed confused by his wanting to see her husband. The conversation that followed was astounding to Roger.

"You knew my husband?" Mrs. Hanover asked, wanting to know more.

Roger told how when he was hitchhiking home after his military service, her husband had given him a ride.

"Can you tell me exactly when that was?" she asked.

"Yes, it was May seventh, the day I was discharged from the army five years ago."

Trying to maintain her composure, Mrs. Hanover asked if something happened that would bring him back after all these years to see her husband.

Roger hesitated. "Well, yes, Mrs. Hanover. I explained the gospel to your husband, and he pulled over to the side of the road and gave his life to Christ. He told me it was the greatest thing that had ever happened to him."

Mrs. Hanover covered her face with her hands and sobbed. "I prayed for my husband's salvation for years. And I believed God would save him," she managed.

"Where is your husband now, Mrs. Hanover?" asked Roger.

"He's dead." She wept again, struggling to speak. "He had an accident that day, evidently after he let you out of the car. He never came home. I thought God hadn't kept His promise." Speaking between sobs, she added, "I stopped living for God five years ago because I thought He hadn't kept His Word!"[3]

There are times in our life when we don't know the direct outcome of our prayers, and the enemy wants us to think that God didn't hear us or didn't care. This is never the case, of course, even if we don't see immediate answers or the outcomes we anticipate. If you were feeling like God doesn't care about you, you might be reading this book to find comfort and know that He does see you. Well, He does, and He is actively working behind the scenes to do what only He can do for you and your loved ones.

When we pray persistently, there is a measure of suffering that comes in the waiting. It is in the dark nights of intercession when forces around us seem to taunt us with words like, "God isn't hearing you!" or "God doesn't care!" or "You will never see change in the person you are praying for."

Those seasons, described by some as the "dark night of the soul," will forge a great testimony if you remain persistent. The fruit borne will bear witness to the goodness of God—if you don't lose heart and continue to press toward your goal in prayer.

Consider the following diary entries in the life of one young Christian servant:

- Sunday a.m. May 5: Preached in St. Anne's. Asked not to come back.
- Sunday p.m.: Preached in St. John's. Deacons said, "Get out, and stay out!"
- Sunday a.m. May 12: Preached in St. Jude's. Can't go back there either.
- Sunday a.m. May 19: Preached in St. Somebody else's. Deacons called special meeting, and said I couldn't return.
- Sunday a.m. May 26: Preached on street. Kicked off street.

- Sunday a.m. June 2: Preached at the edge of town. Kicked off highway.
- Sunday p.m. June 2: Preached in a pasture. Ten thousand came.[4]

These are actual entries from the diaries of John Wesley, one of the greatest revivalists who ever preached. John Wesley's diaries are full of these kinds of stories of persecution and blessing. Like Wesley, there will be times in your life when it seems like nothing you are doing counts for the kingdom and that God isn't listening. Be assured, He is always listening. The end of the teaching from the Luke 18 passage gives us an absolutely wonderful promise:

> And shall not God avenge his own elect, which cry day and night unto him, though he bear long with them?
>
> LUKE 18:7 KJV

The verse goes on to essentially say that He will avenge us speedily. My translation for that: *Suddenly!* I have often found that God is silent for a long time and seems like He isn't answering and then, all of a sudden, the answer comes. I often laugh with my friends and say, "I think God has two speeds—Pause and Fast-Forward!" Or perhaps I could say, wait and suddenly! One thing is certain: God is never early and He is never late.

Perhaps Jesus' most famous parable was when He gave His disciples the Lord's Prayer (Luke 11:2–4). Consider the progression of these verses (i.e., Luke 11:2–4 and then Luke 11:5–8). In other words, first Jesus taught His disciples to pray *Your kingdom come, Your will be done on earth as it is in heaven,* and then He told a parable of persistent prayer so we would know that the kingdom of God will not come without intercession.

What I find reassuring is that in the Lord's Prayer, Jesus gave us a tangible list of things for which to pray. One of those things is our daily needs.

In my book *The Reformation Manifesto,* I mention that the daily need spoken of in this passage is not only personal but can extend to the macro level, for example, to see the elimination of systemic poverty. Give *us* our daily bread can be interpreted to mean a broader sense than merely the individual. The point is that God has answers to both small and large problems and we need to seek Him for them.

One old-fashioned word for persistence is *importunity.* My translation of the word is *shameless persistence.* When we need something from God, we have to be willing to go to Him until we see the answer come.

The Power of Standing in the Gap

Dick Eastman told me a wonderful testimony about the power of persistent prayer while I was talking to him on the phone recently. For those of you who don't know Dick, I call him God's Apostle of Prayer. He is president of Every Home for Christ (EHC), a literature distribution ministry that has blanketed whole nations with the gospel through house-to-house visitation. EHC is seeing as many as 498,000 decisions for Christ from their various offices around the world—in a single month!

Dick Eastman lives in Colorado Springs, Colorado, and lives a life of prayer, even though he is very busy as head of EHC. After moving from the Los Angeles area, Dick and his wife, Dee, purchased a home that had one unique feature—a large space beneath the stairwell. In my mind, this has become a hallowed place in the annals of prayer history, but to Dick it is simply the Gap.

Most of you are probably familiar with Ezekiel 22:30:

> I looked for someone to stand up for me against all this, to repair the defenses of the city, to take a stand for me and stand in the gap to protect this land so I wouldn't have to destroy it. I couldn't find anyone. Not one.
>
> *THE MESSAGE*

Each day that he is home, at some point, Dick goes into his prayer closet. I have looked inside that little room. Among other things, he keeps a little red book there. In it are the writings of Mao Tse Tung, the Communist revolutionary. If you were to examine the book, you would find it is worn with the imprint of Dick's hands. He has held it up to the Lord every day since his trip to Shanghai in 1978—crying out for the salvation of the people of mainland China.

"Dick," I prompted, "tell me about your first visit to Shanghai." I love to listen to his stories, partly because he is a good storyteller, and partly because I am stretched in my faith to pray even more whenever I hear one.

With the tone of voice he uses when he reminisces, he began, "Back in 1978, my friend Jack McAlister and I went to Shanghai for the first time. In those days, we flew to Singapore and then went by ship to Hong Kong, where we booked passage on another ship for Shanghai, China.

"Upon arriving in the harbor, one of the things I noted was that there were no high-rise buildings—only tall billboards of Mao Tse Tung. At that time, God gave me a passion to intercede for revival in China. It was on that trip that I brought home Mao's *Little Red Book.*

"Once home, I put the book in the Gap, as well as felt inspired by the Holy Spirit to pray for every province of China every day."

And indeed, more than thirty years of persistent prayer has seen great fruit. When Dick first went to China he was only a young man accompanying Jack McAlister, and now he is the president of an organization that is impacting all of Asia with the gospel.

If you go to Shanghai today, you will see an entirely different cityscape. High-rises are everywhere, and it is a very modern place. Something else has changed as well—there are many, many believers living there today as well as in every province that Dick has covered with his tears and prayers.

There are times when we seem to stand alone in our prayers. Of course, this is not the case, for God never relies upon one person alone to see His will accomplished through prayer. And of course tens of thousands of Christians (perhaps hundreds of thousands) have been stirred by the Holy Spirit to pray for China on a regular basis. However, I always encourage a person to pray as if they are the only one God is counting on. Like Dick Eastman, we need to be willing to intercede as if we are the only one praying. Rest assured that Jesus understands those moments when we are fighting what seems like every demon in hell as we stand our ground in intercession.

Consider how the Lord must have felt the night before He was betrayed by Judas. The passage found in Matthew 26:36–46 is a profoundly moving study of Jesus, the great intercessor, battling for victory all alone. I quote R. Arthur Matthews in my book *Possessing the Gates of the Enemy* in reference to Jesus in the garden:

The Soldier of the Cross had taught His disciples the need to pray "Thy will be done on earth as it is in heaven." Here (in Gethsemane) He is the lead actor. It is here that He sets Himself to endure the travail pains of demanding prayer warfare and actively wills for God to do His work through Him, regardless of the cost to Himself. His troubled spirit expressed itself in groans, strong crying, and tears. The battle is joined. The intensity mounts. Heaven's legions press forward to help, but this is not their battlefield; it is His alone. His will is assailed at every point. *"And His sweat became like great drops of blood falling down in the ground"* (Luke 22:44). Here is God's work being done in God's way. God wills it in heaven and a man wills it on the earth. The sacrifice at Calvary happened because first, out of His soul's depths in dark Gethsemane, the Soldier of the Cross willed with God for it to happen.[5]

There are moments when we must be persistent in prayer even though every emotion within us wants to quit. Jesus was our example in this. We may be called upon to be persistent, like Dick Eastman, for a nation and people we do not know. It might be our family for whom we are seemingly wrestling against all the hordes of hell. And there are days when we will be distracted, tired, sick, bored, or even downright tired of praying. That's normal; we are, after all, only human. But God has the victory—He just wants our heart and our willingness to pray. He will do the rest!

The good news is that we are not alone in the battle. The Great Warrior, the Lord of Hosts, is fighting alongside us. So don't let your emotions collapse under the strain of fierce warfare. God will give you courage to fight the good fight of faith to see your prayer answered.

Remember the old proverb "It's always darkest before dawn"? This seems to be true in the battle for souls and for nations. It is right before your biggest breakthrough and greatest triumph that the enemy throws his full weight around to knock you out of the battle. Be persistent in prayer! Fight on, and you will win!

Chapter Three

Praying the Will of God

As a little girl, I thought I'd figured out the best way to pray and I had the words practically memorized. My prayers went something like this: *Father God, if it be Thy will, please bring me a new friend. In Jesus' name. Amen.*

Of course at that time we only had the King James Version of the Bible, so I prayed in King James English. Every prayer I uttered had some kind of proviso in it that included a big bold **if it be Thy will.** To my way of thinking, I was letting God be God and make all the decisions. It was also a clause that I think I added just in case God didn't answer my prayer.

What I did not understand at the time was that God had already given me His revealed Word—His answer—for many (or most) of the prayers to which I tagged that very religious-sounding addendum, *if it be Thy will.*

As I reflect on my childish prayers, I understand now that I simply did not realize the Bible gives clear instructions on how to pray the will of God. In fact, one of the most well-known prayers in Scripture commands us to pray His will into the earth: "Your kingdom come. Your will be done on earth as it is in heaven" (Matthew 6:10).

Essentially, I am sure God loved to hear my voice in prayer in my childish recitations, and what I prayed probably accomplished some sort of change. My prayers, however, most likely did little to release the will of God into the situation for which I was praying. I could not pray with faith that my God would bring me a new friend because I felt that I could never really know His will for my life. There are many promises about friendship in the Bible, but I simply did not know how to believe them and apply them to my situation.

Aligning Your Prayers With God's Will

So how does one know how to pray in a way that is aligned with God's will? Quite simply, He has revealed His will through His Word. Since that is true, why do some Christians—as I did as a child—tack an *"if it be Thy will"* on the end of their prayers?

As far as I can discern, this type of pensive *if* praying is based on a seemingly broad theological interpretation of Jesus' prayers in the garden, where three times He cries out to God before His crucifixion: "Not my will but yours be done." (See Matthew 26:39, 42, 44.)

In this passage, Jesus already knew the will of God. In fact, He was born for that momentous day when He would bear the sins of all of us. He came into the world and wrapped himself in flesh to die for the sins of all humankind, and that human flesh was having an enormous battle. His struggle was in *submitting* His flesh to the will of God, not in *discerning* the will of God. Do you ever feel that way? In other words, you *know* the right thing to do in God's eyes (i.e., He's made His will clear to you), but your flesh screams out not to do it (such as fasting, abstaining from a favorite treat, going the extra mile for a neighbor in a bind, etc.).

I must admit that I have from time to time found myself in this kind of struggle with my own will, albeit on a much smaller scale than Christ's battle in the garden of Gethsemane. My human will certainly did not want to accept the call of God on my life. I simply did not want to travel and teach on prayer; rather, I wanted to be a stay-at-home mom—a job I still consider to be one of the greatest honors on earth.

This was not God's plan for me, however. He called me to be both a mother and a prayer leader. My struggle against my own desires and flesh were enormous during this time, as God dealt with me to accept His calling on my life.

If you would permit me to reminisce a bit, I think my story will expand upon the point I am making here.

When I was nine years old, I went forward in a chapel service at the summer camp I was attending. I'll never forget that day. I sang, *"I have decided to follow Jesus, no turning back, no turning back,"* as I walked to the front of that rustic chapel nestled among the pines in Prescott, Arizona. At that time, I dedicated my life to be a missionary.

Life flowed along for me and God's call remained somewhat dormant, although I was very active in my church as a teenager and as a young adult. Later, one year after Mike and I were married, I graduated from Pepperdine University in Malibu, California, with a degree in music education.

From there, life only became busier as we started our life together and then had two children. Finally, on my thirtieth birthday, I remarked to my pastor's wife, "I guess God's calling on my life is to just keep doing what I'm doing right now." Looking back on that statement, I laugh at how wrong I was. Little did I know that a day would come when I would speak every year on each inhabited continent on the planet!

When I turned thirty, we moved from California to Weatherford, Texas. Twenty-one years had passed since that little nine-year-old girl heard God's missionary calling while praying among the Arizona pines. During the ensuing two decades, He had mentioned nothing at all to me about becoming a missionary. And then suddenly He made it clear that now was the time for His calling to come into fulfillment. My flesh rebelled, as every part of my life now seemed settled. It felt like the very fabric of what I thought was my personal identity was being shredded!

The mini-version of the story of that season of my life is this: God's Spirit was telling me something so far beyond my comprehension that I felt like I was having serious delusions! Even though I knew God had called me when I was nine, that episode seemed to me like a distant memory. My will rebelled and I simply did not want to leave my comfort zone. I even tried to get God to call Mike instead of me!

At last, one dark night after wrestling with God, I knelt beside our blue velvet couch and prayed the words that lined me up with God's will for my life, *"Father God, my life is not my own. Here I am, Lord, send me."*

Of course, the long and short of it was that soon after this "couch episode," doors began to fly open to the call of God, and within a few years Mike and I were gathering generals of intercession to pray together across the nations of the earth. I knew the will of God, but my flesh wrestled with it until I at last submitted to the Master of the Universe.

There are times when the will of God may seem uncertain to us and even times when our flesh struggles. But as I mentioned earlier, Scripture reveals His will in many, many cases so that we simply do not have to tag on the line "If it be your will." Isn't it reassuring to know that God has already revealed His will in Scripture?

Finding Our Confidence in Prayer

This leads us to a very important and basic question: "How do I pray according to the will of God and see my prayers answered?" Every person who prays does so in the hope they will receive the answer they desire from God. This is what this chapter is about—teaching you how to pray in God's will to see your prayers answered.

Knowing how important it is to align one's prayers with the will of God, I want to begin with one very important biblical word: *confidence*.

I love this verse:

> Now this is the confidence that we have in Him, that if we ask anything according to His will, He hears us. And if we know that He hears us, whatever we ask, we know that we have the petitions that we have asked of Him.
>
> 1 JOHN 5:14–15

In order to see our prayers answered, we first need to be confident that He wants to answer them! But where does this confidence come from? Can we just *wish* it into existence? That reminds me of a story I once heard relayed to me on the subject of humility. My friend John Dawson, the leader of Youth With a Mission (YWAM), said to a small audience: "On the count of three, I want all of us to be humble: One, two, three—Be humble!" The crowd laughed, of course, because a person can't just decide to be humble. Humility is *born out of an understanding of God's will for our lives*—that humility is acquired through the power of the Holy Spirit as we are transformed into His image. In other words, humility is the fruit of a life submitted to God and His purposes.

And so it is with God's will: We don't just wake up one day and say, "Today's the day—this is the day I am going to gain confidence in God's ability to answer my prayers!" (Wouldn't it be great if God did work that way?!) To illustrate how we can gain the confidence that God will hear and answer our petitions, let me share a story about George Müller, the great nineteenth-century British saint of God who fed thousands of orphans and raised more than a million pounds in his lifetime to help the poor and needy. Müller was a man noted for his confidence in God's ability and willingness to answer his prayers. A great example of Müller's confidence is illustrated by this amazing story, told by the captain of a ship upon which Müller was traveling:

> We had George Müller of Bristol on board. . . . I had been on the bridge for twenty-four hours and never left it, and Müller came to me and said, "Captain, I have come to tell you I must be in Quebec on Saturday afternoon."
>
> "It is impossible," I said.
>
> "Then very well, if your ship cannot take me, God will find some other way. I have never broken an engagement in fifty-seven years; let us go down into the chart room and pray."
>
> I looked at the man of God and thought to myself, *What lunatic asylum can that man have come from, for I have never heard of such a thing as this.* "Müller," I said, "Do you know how dense this fog is?"
>
> "No," he replied, "My eye is not on the density of the fog, but on the living God who controls every circumstance of my life." He knelt down and prayed one of the simplest prayers.
>
> When he finished, I was going to pray, but he put his

hand on my shoulder and told me not to pray. "As you do not believe He will answer, and as I believe He has, there is no need whatever for you to pray about it."

I looked at him, and George Müller said, "Captain, I have known my Lord for fifty-seven years and there has never been a single day when I have failed to get an audience with the King. Get up, Captain, and open the door, and you will find the fog has gone."

I got up, and the fog indeed was gone, and on that Saturday afternoon George Müller kept his promised engagement.[1]

Müller was confident in God because he knew that God had called him to speak in Quebec; he knew that God would move heaven and earth to get him to Quebec if he only believed and prayed with confidence. He did not doubt that what he asked of God he would receive *because he knew what he was asking was God's will.* He did not pray an if-it-be-Thy-will prayer. He already knew His will.

And that, my friends, is the key: When we study His Word, and God reveals His will, we can be confident that God will see it done. So our confidence is not in our own ability to discern His will, but in God's ability to reveal it to us! Put another way, once we understand His revealed will through His Word, we can be confident in how to pray and see our prayers answered. For instance, His Word says that He will supply all of our needs according to His riches in glory by Christ Jesus (Philippians 4:19). We don't have to ask if it is His will to feed our family or keep the lights turned on in our house. Therefore, we can confidently ask for provision for these things without tacking an "if it be your will" on the end of it.

How precious that kind of confidence must be to the Lord!

I looked up the dictionary definition of the word *confidence,* and here is what I found:

> Full trust; belief in the powers, trustworthiness, or reliability of a person. Related words: assurance, authority. Antonym: mistrust[2]

We need to pray with full trust and assurance that God wants to answer prayers that are prayed in alignment with His Word and will for our lives.

When Mike and I lived in Weatherford, there was an elderly man named Campbell Walker who lived across the street. Campbell often regaled us with stories of the area when it was the Wild West and the cowboys rode their horses to church. It seems there was a time when the whole region was in a terrible drought. The pastor called a special session of prayer to cry out to God for rain. To his surprise, one young cowboy came striding down the aisle, carrying his saddle, no doubt his stirrups making loud clanking sounds as he walked.

"Cowboy," the pastor said, "Why are you bringing your saddle into the house of the Lord?"

"Well, pastor," he drawled in his Texas accent, "We came to pray for rain; this is my new saddle and I don't want it to get wet!"[3]

The young cowboy had faith. He wasn't there to ask God to send rain and wonder if the Lord would answer—he believed that what he asked in prayer was possible and that as a result rain was imminent.

It is totally possible to pray according to the already revealed will of God and expect our prayers to be answered. If one young cowboy could have that kind of faith, we can too. We should pray with complete confidence, authority, and trust that He will do what we ask Him to do for us.

The Privilege of Prayer

Prayer is an interesting thing. In principle, because God is all-powerful, He could do anything He wants at any time without our involvement. However, author and prayer leader Bob Willhite says, "The law of prayer is the highest law of the universe—it can overcome the other laws by sanctioning God's intervention."[4]

God established the law of prayer as the governing force for His will to be done in heaven as it is on earth, and He therefore chose to partner with us to see it done. We don't have to ask if God wants His will done on earth as it is in heaven because we know by reading Matthew 6:10 that He does.

Why pray if we are only praying God's will back to Him? Such a question, of course, tries to unravel the mystery of divine sovereignty and human responsibility. Yet without being able to solve that mystery, we can answer the real issue it poses. The answer is relatively straightforward: God in His sovereignty has chosen to work His will through human prayer. It appears that God has chosen not to do what He might like to do if human beings refuse to pray for it. On the one hand, He mixes prayer with privilege. Christians are invited to work together with the Creator of the universe. If a believer does not correctly perceive the will of God, God is not bound to answer that prayer.[5]

Here are some of the things we know with certainty that God wants accomplished on the earth:

1. He wants nations to be discipled according to a biblical worldview.
2. He wants us to teach nations according to His revealed Word. (Matthew 28:19–20)
3. He wants us to fulfill the role for which we were created,

and so He has limited His involvement in the earth; instead, He calls for our intercession for His will to be done.

My friend Dutch Sheets aptly explains this in his excellent book *Authority in Prayer*:

> What God intended for Adam was intended for all adams, including authority over the earthly realm. This is why Genesis 1:26 says, "God made man (adam) in His image and then said 'let them rule.' " All adams, the entire human race, were given authority over the earth.
>
> Psalm115:16 confirms God's original intent concerning humankind's dominion mandate: "The heavens are the heavens of the Lord but the earth He has given to the sons of men (adam)." This verse's "given" comes from a Hebrew word that can mean ownership but also means "to give in the sense of an assignment," it means "to put in charge of."[6] God was saying to us adamites, "I'll take charge of the stars, planets, and galaxies, but the earth is yours—you're in charge of it." This is why James Moffat, in his translation of Scriptures, renders that portion, "the earth He has assigned to men." God didn't give away the rulership of the earth, but He did assign humans the responsibility of governing or stewarding it, *starting with our private world* and continuing to our extended and universal ones.[7]

I italicized the words "starting with our private world" because this is where we, as believers, must begin in our walk of faith as we learn to exercise our authority in prayer. Going back to the title of this chapter, the first premise we need to be completely clear about is that God wants us to claim the promises He has already given and pray them with confidence.

Standing on the Promises of God

As a little girl, our church always sang the hymn "Standing on the Promises." This always puzzled me a bit as I pondered with my childish mind: *God, do you want me to stand on top of my Bible?*

How does one stand on the promises of God? First of all, find a Scripture that pertains to your situation and find the promise in it. Some promises are broad-sweeping in scope and cover a wide range of needs, such as this one:

> Therefore I say to you, whatever things you ask when you pray, believe that you receive them, and you will have them.
>
> MARK 11:24

Another great verse that I often quote and use to "stand on the promise" is:

> Whatever you ask the Father in My name He will give you. Until now you have asked nothing in My name. Ask, and you will receive, that your joy may be full.
>
> JOHN 16:23–24

Of course this asking must be contingent upon our praying in a way that is consistent with God's nature and character and not reflective of our own selfish wishes. I heard of a little child who was so jealous of his new baby sister that he asked God to take her back to heaven! It isn't hard to discern that such a churlish prayer is not in accordance with the will of God! Why? It is God who gives life and He doesn't leave it up to the whim of a jealous child to determine his sibling's destiny through a prayer.

As I grow and learn to stand upon the promises of God, I have gained great comfort and inspiration from reflecting on

His names in the Bible. Here are a few of God's names, available to us as we pray, knowing that He will answer us according to His divine nature:

1. **Jehovah-Jireh**/Genesis 22:14—He is our provider, and there are many precious promises from God that He will provide for us as we pray in His name.
2. **Jehovah-Rapha** /Isaiah 53:5—He is the One who heals. We call upon Him and ask for healing through this name and with the understanding of this attribute of God.
3. **Jehovah-Nissi**/Exodus 17:15—God is our protector or banner.
4. **Jehovah-Shalom**/Judges 6:24—He is the God of peace who helps us in the midst of life's storms.

In addition, there are names of God (or aspects of who He is) that we can call upon in our prayers, such as:

1. **The God of All Comfort**/2 Corinthians 1:3
2. **Lord of the Harvest**/Luke 10:2
3. **The God of Mercy**/Luke 1:78

You Don't Need to Pray Alone

One of the best ways to discover God's will is to garner prayers from others who are adept at hearing His voice in intercession. If possible, turn to those who know you best, care about your destiny, and are aligned in mind and spirit with you and your situation. And if possible, elicit prayer from your pastor or other leaders of your church to whom you have access, or other authority figures in your life.

In the early 1990s, Mike and I were thinking about moving to Colorado Springs, so I called my friend Dick Eastman, who lived in the city, to get his opinion. Without knowing what I was calling for, this great man of prayer, who has interceded for our family for years, started telling me that he believed the Lord was assembling "generals of prayer" to intercede for the city. Of course, this was quite meaningful to me, because as you may know, the name of our ministry is Generals International (at that time the name was actually Generals of Intercession).

Our next step in the decision-making process was to seek the counsel of our board of directors, which at the time included leaders like Dutch Sheets, Peter Wagner, and others. All concurred that moving to Colorado Springs was the right thing to do.

In fact, Peter Wagner, who was living in the Pasadena, California, area at the time, also made the move to Colorado Springs shortly after we did.

Many other people prayed with us and we received almost all favorable responses. The few friends who did not support our move had a vested emotional interest in our staying in Texas.

Then ten years later, our friend Sam Brassfield, an intercessor who has spoken powerfully into our life over the years, called and told us he believed God wanted us to move back to Texas. To say we were shocked was an understatement! In fact, at the time I quipped to a close associate, "Couldn't God have just said, 'Don't go' the first time, so we wouldn't have had to move twice?!" I guess God had a plan for us to be nomadic intercessors or else missionaries to Colorado Springs for a season.

Moving for us is quite complicated; by that time our staff had grown since leaving Texas and we owned a good deal more equipment than when we had originally moved to Colorado Springs. Mike and I had also purchased eight beautiful wooded acres for the dream home we wanted to build. All our bills were paid off and we were doing well financially.

We started to pray and asked many to pray with us. We met with a group of close, prayer-minded friends, and as we prayed they all—to a person!—confirmed that it was God's will for us to move back to Texas.

At last, we met with our board—the same one who had given God's stamp of approval, as it were, for us to move to Colorado—and one of them, prayer leader and author Chuck Pierce, prophesied in prayer that we were to move back in five months. *Five months!* We almost fainted! God wasn't making this easy.

Five months later, however, the moving vans pulled out of Colorado Springs loaded with desks, media equipment, and all of our worldly goods. Our return to Texas has been a great blessing, as *God knows* the right place where our destiny will advance. And that is His desire for you too: to be able to recognize and seize upon His will, so that the favor of God will rest upon your life. [8]

Chapter Four

Blockages to Answered Prayer

While on the road to seeing answers to long-standing prayers, it is critical to understand the types of blockages that can threaten your progress. In some cases, life throws us some curve balls and we run the risk of becoming shipwrecked (1 Timothy 1:19). This was the case for my younger sister, Lucy.

Even though we grew up in a Christian home, my little sister had some challenges in her faith. Our daddy's sudden death at the age of forty-nine truly rocked Lucy's boat of faith. Dad died when Lucy was sixteen, and while I am not saying that his death was the only reason Lucy struggled with her faith, his death didn't help.

Lucy and I have always been close. She is five years younger than me, and when she was born I thought she was the most beautiful little creation I had ever seen. Her hair was curly and blond, and if you pulled those little curls they would spring back like a corkscrew.

One day she met Mark, a handsome blue-eyed guy from Minnesota who was visiting San Antonio, Texas, along with his buddy Glenn. And while Lucy's best friend, Beatrice, fell in love with Glenn, my sister fell in love with Mark. Subsequently, Mark and Lucy married and began their life together. The only problem was that she wasn't the least bit interested in following the Lord. And while Mark was a good man, he wasn't a Christian, which gave Lucy even less incentive to return to her faith.

Soon after Lucy was married, I started a letter-writing campaign, thinking I could lecture her into the kingdom of God. At the end of my letters to my sis, I would always include a list of Scriptures. She later told me that she just threw the letters in the trash. (Ouch—all that time looking up all those verses!)

At last I got smart and started taking both Mark's and Lucy's cases before the greatest and wisest convincer and author of conviction in the universe—the Holy Spirit.

My sister, Lucy, was not the person she had been taught to be growing up.

The parable of the prodigal son (Luke 15:11–31) addresses behavior that runs contrary to what a person has been raised to believe and underscores the transformation that God brings when a person has an encounter with Him. A friend just pointed out something to me that I had never noticed in the story of the prodigal son:

> But when he *came to himself,* [the prodigal son] said, "How many of my father's hired servants have bread enough and to spare, and I perish with hunger!"
>
> LUKE 15:17

My sister was not acting like herself! By nature and upbringing, she was created to serve and love God. She had been taught about Jesus from the moment she was brought into this world. The reason she was not acting like herself was because she was burdened by the hurts and pains of life, or "the cares of this world" (Matthew 13:22).

As I interceded for my sister, I realized that she needed to be healed of the pain of losing our dad as well as from other things that had happened in her life. I asked God for a strategy in prayer to see her healing become a reality. And then, little by little, I could tell that God was restoring Lucy's soul. At last, after six years of intercession, Lucy called me to say that she had rededicated her life to the Lord. Here is her testimony of how it happened:

> One day while I was away from the Lord I turned on the television set to a Christian television program. To my surprise, a man came on and said, "The Holy Spirit tells me there is a woman watching the show and she has been away from the Lord and is trying to come back."
>
> With those words, the power of God hit me and knocked me to my knees. There was no doubt in my mind that it was the Lord, himself, who was visiting me right there in my living room.

The blockage was removed as Lucy felt the love and conviction of the Lord—suddenly (as God often works!) my little sister *came to herself once again.* In a short span of time she had a supernatural transformation from the bondage of spiritual darkness as she walked freely back into the everlasting arms of the Savior. She later went forward at my mother's church in Texas and officially rededicated her life to the Lord.

Dramatic, huh? God is quite convincing in His dealings with sinners. If you think that story is amazing, just wait until I share how God got hold of Mark, her scientifically minded husband. His story fits into another category of blockages to unanswered prayer, which I will relay shortly.

The story of the struggle my sister had after the death of our dad has probably been repeated in households across the face of the earth for hundreds of years. If this is a variation of a story of one of your own family members, do not give up: There will be a day when they will wake up and "come to themselves" once again!

Let's look at different blockages, one by one, so we can understand how to get the breakthrough in prayer that we all desire and to see our prayers answered.

Blockage #1: A Deep Emotional Wound

Deep emotional wounds (like the one that inflicted my sister) are some of the most common blockages that can keep people from responding to the Lord's voice of love. One key when we are interceding for a loved one is to determine what the root issue is and tailor a prayer strategy to deal with it.

At times the trauma that has thrown a person into a prodigal state is evident; other times it may be more obscure. There are times when I have prayed for someone but have had difficulty identifying the blockage(s) that inhibits that person's return to the Lord. I have listed here various ways to discover the particular root to a person's problem(s):

A. Listen to the person's conversation. Do they talk about all the "hypocrites" in the church? They probably have been either wounded or jaded by some kind of interaction either with established religion or a Christian leader. If you believe this to be the case, ask God to send laborers along their path who are not hypocritical and will restore them to seeing true Christianity.

B. Believe that the Lord will reveal to the person, or to others, their pain through a dream or vision.

C. Hurt and trauma can cause us to be shipwrecked in our faith and in our prayers. First Timothy 1:19 says, "Having faith and a good conscience, which some having rejected, concerning the faith have suffered shipwreck."

It isn't hard to spot someone who has been shipwrecked by life in general. They were hurt at a certain point in time by some traumatic episode and afterward struggled to grow spiritually. Very often when that point of hurt or trauma is healed, they will leave the shores of pain and become alive again in Christ.

The gift of prophecy is a very powerful tool when praying for someone who has been spiritually shipwrecked. There have been times when I have been ministering to someone in prayer and the Lord has pinpointed a moment of pain in that person's past, revealed it, and then brought comfort and healing.

One particularly startling example occurred at the end of a church service when I asked a young couple to step into the aisle to receive prayer. The woman jumped up eagerly, but the man stood up slowly and followed rather reluctantly. In fact, he had what appeared to me to be a cloak of shame on his shoulders.

I looked at him and asked if he had an anger problem. At first he blustered and deferred, so I reached out my hand and prayed forcefully for him to be freed from his anger. At first it looked like the man had been struck by lightning, but then his face began to shine in a glorious manner.

The young couple told me after the service that they had been separated for a couple of months due to his anger issues.

He had a propensity to become enraged and violent to the point of beating his wife. The day I met them was the first Sunday they had been back together, and he had spent quite a bit of the night before crying out to the Lord to set him free from his violent anger problem.

If you know of someone who has been shipwrecked by life's storms, don't give up praying for them. God is able to heal them and bring deliverance in ways beyond your imagination.

Blockage #2: Unforgiveness

Unforgiveness is probably the most common blockage or hindrance to answered prayer. Not only is it a blockage, but it often keeps us from the place of prayer and private devotion.

Recently I noticed that I didn't have the desire to get up and pray as much as I normally do. I used the excuse, "I'm tired and I've been traveling a lot, so I need to sleep more." Of course that *is* true! Being tired, however, didn't keep me from the other essentials in my day, like eating when I was hungry, drinking when I was thirsty, etc. At last the Holy Spirit penetrated my heart in His wonderful wooing way and whispered, "Cindy, why aren't you spending more time with me?"

If you are married, you might relate to the next statement: I have noticed that if Mike hurts my feelings, I tend to withdraw. We may not be fighting, but I just don't go the second mile with him as much in our relationship. Eventually we either talk about it or I will realize that I was simply being oversensitive (and get over it on my own). This kind of situation can happen in one's relationship with the Lord as well, and that was what happened in my case. The reason? A good friend of mine died after I had prayed persistently for her to be healed. I was hurt over her death and perhaps even a bit mad at God. Of course, Satan was delighted that I wasn't getting up and standing in the gap as much. This meant that the enemy's kingdom could advance more because I wasn't on the wall in intercessory prayer—or someone else had to take up my slack!

What did I do? I repented. It is interesting how repentance works: Before one does it, for some reason, it seems so difficult; but afterward, a person usually thinks, *What took me so long?* The lag is usually because of our pride. Ed Silvoso says that pride is like bad breath—you're the last one to know you have it!

Unforgiveness causes other blockages to prayer as well. Mark 11:25-26 is a great Scripture on unforgiveness and repentance:

> And whenever you stand praying, if you have anything against anyone, forgive him, that your Father in heaven may also forgive you your trespasses. But if you do not forgive, neither will your Father in heaven forgive your trespasses.

Another key verse that goes along with this one is Psalm 66:18:

> If I regard iniquity in my heart, the Lord will not hear me.
>
> KJV

Many times we become upset with God in prayer because we think He isn't listening or that He is uncaring. Of course nothing could be further from the truth! It is against His nature to be anything but a kind, listening Father. He has set up certain laws, however, that govern answered prayer, and even He will not violate them because of His righteousness. And when we hold on to unforgiveness it has its consequences:

Listen now! The Lord isn't too weak to save you! And he isn't getting deaf! He can hear you when you call! But the trouble is that your sins have cut you off from God. Because of sin he has turned his face away from you and will not listen anymore.

ISAIAH 59:1–2 TLB

Further, unforgiveness is a two-edged sword. It can both keep our prayers from being answered as we intercede for a person or stop the person we are praying for from being able to hear the voice of God.

As I mentioned earlier, it is possible to have unforgiveness in one's life and not even be aware of the problem. And because we normally don't run around thinking things like, "I hate that person!" or "I will never forgive them for what they did to me," we think we are fine. This is why it is important to regularly check in with the Lord and make sure you are not harboring some root of bitterness against anyone without recognizing it. The ship of life passing through troubled waters can pick up some hitchhiking barnacles of unforgiveness without our even being aware that they have attached themselves to our emotions. The Lord also wants us to stay accountable to loved ones or Christian friends, as He uses good counselors in our life to help us remain "barnacle-free."

It is hard to intercede for a person toward whom we harbor bitterness. Try it sometime: Every time we try to pray, the trespass against us (or against someone we care about) pops up in our thinking. In order to check for hidden areas of unforgiveness, many people pray and meditate on Matthew 6:14–15:

For if you forgive men their trespasses, your heavenly Father will also forgive you. But if you do not forgive men their trespasses, neither will your Father forgive your trespasses.

Blockage #3: Bitter Roots

This brings us to the biblical question, "If we pray to forgive by faith, is it a done deal?" In other words, have we really forgiven? I personally believe God sees our heart the moment we move to forgive by faith. We should not stop there, however, but continue to intercede until the pain and trauma of those hurtful experiences is dealt with completely. If we do not continue in our personal intercession until we are completely free from the residue, it is possible that we can still develop roots of bitterness.

Roots of bitterness damage our ability to properly hear the voice of God; they also make it difficult to discern how and when He wants us to intercede for a person or situation. Our very prayers can be defiled by bitterness, wherein our hurt and pain can keep us from interceding for a person for whom God wants us to pray. We need to pursue the words found in Hebrews:

> Looking diligently lest any man fail of the grace of God; lest any root of bitterness springing up trouble you, and thereby many be defiled.
>
> HEBREWS 12:15 KJV

The other night in prayer the Lord shocked me by asking me to intercede for a Christian leader who had tried to cause great damage against me and our ministry. He called me a false prophet, and it seemed that almost everywhere I went he spoke slander against me.

Frankly, even before this, during the time when he was saying these things, I did pray on a regular basis to forgive him. My morning prayers went something like this: *"And Lord, I forgive him again!"* At the end of the day I stopped and thought, *Hmmm, forgiven that minister again for what I heard today? Check!*

I wasn't at all surprised when I heard a new report of his vitriol and bitter lies about me. One day, however, I decided that enough was enough. I made a plan to call two major Christian leaders who knew us both well and have them decide whether or not I was the wolf in sheep's clothing this man was claiming me to be.

Feeling quite righteous about my decision, I called a friend and tried to tell him of my masterful plan. "Now Cindy," he said, "do you really want to divide the body of Christ by doing that?"

Body of Christ! I thought, *What about me? Don't I count in this equation? Doesn't it matter that I have feelings too?*

The whole conversation set me to fuming again about the injustice done against me. Later I whined, *"Lord, I confronted that guy about his sexual sin, and now he is out to destroy me. Do something to defend me!"* I was also hurt and a bit mad that the friend I called had not jumped to my defense!

In life there are moments when it is quite difficult to practice what one preaches—and that was my case at that time. On countless occasions I had shared with others, "You can't hurt God's reputation. If you are relying on your own reputation, it will never see you through the trials of ministry. Give your reputation to God and die to yourself."

Good preaching, Cindy, but hard advice to follow.

I should have known that I was going to get the spanking from God that I greatly deserved, and sure enough, the next morning the Holy Spirit was waiting for me. During my quiet time with the Lord I opened my Bible to read and, oh boy, the chastisement began! Here is the Scripture from my reading for the day:

You're familiar with the old written law, "Love your friend," and its unwritten companion, "Hate your enemy." I'm challenging that. I'm telling you to love your enemies. Let them bring out the best in you, not the worst. When someone gives you a hard time, respond with the energies of prayer for then you are working out of your true selves, your God-created selves. This is what God does. He gives His best—the sun to warm and the rain to nourish—to everyone, regardless: the good and bad, the nice and nasty. If all you do is love the lovable, do you expect a bonus? Anybody can do that. If you simply say hello to those who greet you, do you expect a medal? Any run-of-the mill sinner can do that.

In a word, what I'm saying is, *Grow up*. You're kingdom subjects. Now live like it.

MATTHEW 5:43–48 *THE MESSAGE*

God was saying to me that I needed to grow up into a mature believer. I became thoroughly repentant, at which point the Lord went even deeper and said to me, "Cindy Jacobs, you really do not understand the message of the cross at all! You don't fathom how I could pray, 'Father forgive them' on behalf of the very ones who were crucifying me."

I knew that what the Lord was saying was very, very true. I did not begin to fathom the message of the cross. My roots of bitterness had defiled me and had pushed me from my place of intercession before the throne to the point of self-justification. From that day, I began to fervently intercede for that person and still do so to this day, when the Lord prompts me.

This brings me to an important prayer axiom that I learned from the great apostle of prayer Dick Eastman: "My prayer life will never rise above my personal life in Jesus Christ."[1]

Bitterness keeps us from praying undefiled prayers that produce the answers and results we are seeking from God through our intercession.

Blockage #4: Unconfessed Sin

Unconfessed sin often keeps us from spending time in prayer, and much of the time we are unaware that it is the problem. As I mentioned earlier, there are times when we are upset with God and would rather not talk with Him in prayer. Even more, we unconsciously know that if we get in a quiet place with God, we might have to give up an aspect of sin in our life.

At other times, while we desire to have a satisfying conversation with the Lord, we find that we don't have much to say to Him. We just sit there with a blank mind—not able to pray at all.

This is why it is so necessary to have regular times of quiet introspection before the Lord. In such times, we must allow the Holy Spirit to reveal to us any blockages to prayer, especially those related to unconfessed sin.

As Dick Eastman has said, "If we do not take time to wait on the Lord and confess any breaches in our relationship with Him, then an awareness of our past failures tends to buffet the mind as we pray. Suddenly we feel hopelessly unworthy of offering our petitions. The devil has gained a victory, and soon we stop praying altogether."[2]

Isn't it good to know that God is faithful and just to cleanse us from all unrighteousness? (1 John 1:9). Many have likened confession to spiritual surgery: It is painful at the time, but afterward we feel clean and whole with the cancer of sin removed.

I personally love James 5:16:

> Admit your faults to one another and pray for each other that you may be healed. The earnest prayer of a righteous man has great power and wonderful results.
>
> TLB

It is easy for us to quote the last portion of that passage that gives the promise of great power and wonderful results, but we also have moments where we need to admit our faults to others so our prayers will not be hindered. We may not look upon the inability to confess our faults as sin, but at the root of this problem is the sin of spiritual pride.

There comes a moment in everyone's life when they have to leave the place of prayer and make a phone call to ask forgiveness of someone. The difficult part is that the person to whom we are humbling ourselves may not extend forgiveness, or accept ours! Even though this may occur, we still will have cleared our conscience before the Lord and can afterward expect our prayers to be answered with great power. God will continue to deal with the unforgiveness on the part of the other person.

The practice of asking for forgiveness is one of the most powerful and biblical spiritual exercises in which a Christian can partake. Usually the most mature person in a relationship will be the first to repent. It doesn't come down to who has the greatest sin; it is the relationship itself that is of great value.

Our grandsons are little stairsteps in age. Boys all tend to want to be "king of the hill," as we say here in the U.S. Whenever they are fighting, it is often difficult to ascertain who the real culprit is in a given situation.

Usually it starts with one of the boys saying, "Nonnie, he hit me!" At this point, it takes all of my spiritual discernment to determine who really hit whom and which one is the real victim. Often by the time they call me in to referee, all I see is a mass of little bodies in a heap on the floor punching one another. I have to admit that even though there are moments when I can be quite discerning, my gift seems not to operate well when I am in the Nonnie role! After breaking up the fight and looking for scratches and bruises, I work at trying to be fair and getting down to the bottom of the situation.

Usually I find there is room for each of them to ask forgiveness at some level, as I try to teach them to take ownership of their individual reactions. I think by having each own up to his part, it contributes to his spiritual growth.

As followers of Christ, we are like my squabbling grandsons on many levels; few of us can remain blameless in every conflict we encounter. Put another way, we are complicit in some manner either by our actions or responses to the confrontations and stressful situations of life. All of us can grow in our ability to become godlier in our actions. While the situation may not have elevated to a point where we are actually in sin, we can grow in fellowship with the Lord so that the fruit of the Spirit is manifested in the midst of a challenging circumstance.

After I finished writing the last paragraph, I took stock of my own life and sensed a need for improvement in allowing the Holy Spirit to manifest himself through me in the fruits of the Spirit—especially in the area of patience!

Blockage #5: Strongholds of the Mind

One of the biggest blockages to answered prayer comes from strongholds of the mind. Such strongholds (or faulty ways of thinking) can rest both in the person interceding and in the person for whom we are interceding. I like the definition Ed Silvoso uses to describe a stronghold:

> A stronghold is a mindset filled with hopelessness that accepts as unchangeable something that he or she knows is contrary to the will of God.

I would define a stronghold as anything that resists the will of God from being done on the earth as it is in heaven. Both of these together give a pretty complete definition.

I like the way *The Amplified Bible* presents our ability to deal with these kinds of blockages to prayer:

> For the weapons of our warfare are not physical [weapons of flesh and blood], but they are mighty before God for the overthrow and destruction of strongholds, [inasmuch as we] refute arguments and theories and reasonings and every proud and lofty thing that sets itself up against the [true] knowledge of God; and we lead every thought and purpose away captive into the obedience of Christ (the Messiah, the Anointed One).
>
> 2 CORINTHIANS 10:4–5 AMP

There are many strongholds of the mind that assault our thinking as we come before the Lord to pray on behalf of a person or situation. In the next section, we will examine some of them.

Mistrust in the Goodness of God

Mistrust in intercession is when we do not really believe that God wants to answer our prayers. It's critical when we are struggling in such a way that we stop and allow the Holy Spirit to illuminate any faulty or negative thinking, and surrender emotions that might keep us from praying in faith.

Of course if we have suffered disappointments when we felt we had prayed in faith, this could be at the bottom of our inability to believe God. We need to refocus on the fact that God wants the best for both us and the person for whom we are interceding.

Years ago, I was having a hard time praying in faith and was feeling very depressed. I finally asked the Lord to show me what was wrong. This is what I received from the Lord: "Cindy, depression is frozen anger. You are very angry at me over past circumstances in your life."

"Nice Christian girls" are not supposed to get angry (yeah, right!), so I was totally unaware that I was so upset with both God and my past. But as I prayed further, I came to realize that my anger flowed out of deep disappointments in my past. Quite simply, I had expected certain things to go a certain direction in my life, and that had not happened. As I look back today at some of these disappointments, I know that many of them would not even bother me today. At the time, however, due to my level of spiritual maturity, they seemed enormous and all-important.

To move beyond my anger, I asked the Lord to help me make a list of the expectations and dreams I had that I thought should have been fulfilled by that juncture in my life. Slowly but surely, I began to release them to God. I realized that some of the expectations on my list didn't happen because of choices other people had made. And of course some of the unfulfilled dreams involved choices I had made. As I came to each point on the list, I would stop and if need be, grieve a moment. In some cases I actually broke down and wept and then gave those things to God.

One of the biggest issues for me was dealing with the aftermath of losing my dad when he was only forty-nine. I grieved over the fact that he was not there when I married Mike or at the births of our children and grandchildren.

The fact that my pastor daddy was not there for my wedding was particularly hard, because for most of my life we had a sweet family joke. It went like this:

"Daddy, are you going to marry me?" I would ask.

He would respond, "Honey, I'm already married; you'll have

to ask your mom!" When Dad died one month before my wedding, it was a very big heartbreak for me. Yet that was life, and life happens—right? Well, for me, it was just flat-out wrong— *very, very wrong!*

As I prayed and wept again over the loss of both my dad and that little girl's dream, I felt sweetness come into my heart. Another important thing happened as well: Full trust in my heavenly Father was restored. This added a level of confidence to my prayer life that was not there before.

This point leads to a critical factor in our intercessory walk with God: If we do not believe that God is good, then we can't pray in faith expecting Him to do good things for us through answers to our prayers.

Here are some specific ways to pray against the strongholds that come through loss of expectations:

1. Spend time meditating on Scripture and ask the Holy Spirit to show you any unhealed areas where losses or unfulfilled expectations have affected your thinking. In this regard, meditate on Proverbs 3:5–6:

   Lean on, trust in, and be confident in the Lord with all your heart and mind and do not rely on your own insight or understanding. In all your ways know, recognize, and acknowledge Him, and He will direct and make straight and plain your paths.

   AMP

2. Make a list of the things the Lord shows you.

3. Set aside an uninterrupted time of prayer. Make this a top priority in your life. It is interesting how we make time for meals, going to the doctor for physical check-ups, and taking our cars in for regular tune-ups, but

we sometimes shirk spending time going to Jesus for a spiritual tune-up! I know it can be brutally difficult to slip away in prayer even for a day, especially if you are a single parent or work full time. However, it is possible! Call for favors from family, friends, or church members to baby-sit or otherwise "hold down the fort" while you get away for a day or even an overnight. Spending time with God gives us a new level of trust and faith to know that our prayers will be answered.

Strongholds of Wrong Beliefs

We have explored an aspect where a stronghold in the person praying can be a blockage or hindrance to prayer. Of course, strongholds can also exist in the person or situation that is the object of our intercession. Aspects of this subject will be woven throughout the book, but I would like to deal with one wrong set of beliefs now.

What we believe makes up our worldview: how we see the world around us, how we think it should operate, and how we think people should act and believe. And how we view the world has a great deal to do with the way we were educated (i.e., with our educational systems). To put it succinctly, how we were taught greatly influences the way we think. Here in the U.S., particularly in the past fifty years, our educational system has been empirically based, placing high value on scientific thinking over spiritual understanding. Thus we don't always view the world through a spiritual grid or reality. Our culture tends to dismiss or downplay the power of the supernatural in favor of scientifically based truths. Such thinking can not only limit the power of God to move in one's life but also cause us (even inadvertently) to doubt His ability to do so.

When a person is raised in a scientifically driven environment, his "spiritual IQ" can suffer. Less exposure to the things of God makes it more difficult to stay spiritually aware and attuned. And our enemy, Satan, loves spiritual ignorance. In order to deal with and pull down these types of spiritual blockages in people's minds, we need to understand that we have mighty weapons of warfare at our disposal. We also need to do a spiritual diagnosis of the situation by asking the Lord to reveal to us roots of wrong thinking in the person's mind.

Sadly, many Christians, and intercessors, are ignorant of how to deal with the schemes Satan has set up in people's minds. We cannot pray persistent prayers that get results without taking care of our ignorance factor! Not only that, but we are commanded in Scripture not to be ignorant of these schemes.

In his bestselling book *Intercessory Prayer*, Dutch Sheets points out the warning God gives us in Scripture concerning not being ignorant of the enemy's devices. Dutch refers to the *New American Standard* translation to make his point:

> Our ignorance of Satan and his tactics, as well as how to deal with them, is costly for us. Second Corinthians 2:11 tells us: "In order that no advantage be taken of us by Satan; for we are not ignorant of his schemes." The context is forgiveness, but a general principle is also revealed in this verse. The word "ignorant" is the Greek word agnoeo. It means without knowledge or understanding of.[3] Our English word "agnostic" is derived from it. We also get the word "ignore" from the same root. In this verse we're urged not to ignore or be an agnostic—without understanding—where the devil is concerned.[4]

Dutch goes on to explain that we must not be ignorant because Satan will take advantage of us if we are.

My friend, Satan will not only take advantage of us if we are ignorant but he will also take advantage of those we love and those for whom we are praying. In fact, many or most of the people we are interceding for have already been taken advantage of by Satan's schemes! Knowing that God doesn't want us to be "agnostic" or ignorant of Satan's devices, it makes sense that the devil would plant agnostic thoughts in the minds of those we love. These agnostic thoughts are demonically inspired fiery darts shot into their thinking. Such erroneous thoughts lead people to doubt that Jesus is God or that God is indeed real.

The Weapons of Binding and Loosing

How do we war against these imaginations put into a person's mind? Rest assured that these fortresses can be demolished, and God has given us the "siege tools" to bring them down. One powerful tool for demolishing strongholds is found in the biblical principle of binding and loosing. I wrote extensively about this subject in my book *Possessing the Gates of the Enemy*, but will briefly cover it here, as it is such an important tool in dealing with agnosticism. Here is the anchor verse on the subject:

> Assuredly, I say to you, whatever you bind on earth will be bound in heaven, and whatever you loose on earth will be loosed in heaven. Again I say to you that if two of you agree on earth concerning anything that they ask, it will be done for them by My Father in heaven.
>
> Matthew 18:18–19

In essence, "binding" is warfare prayer that comes against something that is not of God, and "loosing" is praying for the full fruit and flow of the Holy Spirit into a situation.

First of all, realize that there are strongholds of agnosticism that must be bound in order to restore the person's ability to hear the voice of God wooing them and revealing His truth. Satan blinds the mind of those who should believe (2 Corinthians 4:4) so they cannot see the light or truth of the gospel.

Here is what a binding prayer would look like in this case:

> Jesus, I bind the enemy in this situation, and I say, in the name of Jesus, you are forbidden to blind the eyes and understanding of _____ through agnosticism, from being able to see the glorious truth of the gospel.

There are times when the stronghold is deeply entrenched and the battle in prayer will take more than one weapon of warfare. As Jesus points out in Mark 29:9, sometimes it is critical to mix our prayers with a time of fasting. I will cover this more extensively in the next chapter as we broaden our study of persistent prayer through learning the authority we have through Christ in prayer.

We all have friends and loved ones who struggle with agnostic thoughts, including those who are blinded to the truth that Jesus is God or who fail to believe that Jesus is the only way to heaven. As you pray for these loved ones, I encourage you in the path of persistence, praying that they would turn to Christ and see the truth, even through what seems to be a very long season. This was true in the case of my brother-in-law, Mark.

Mark came from a Presbyterian background. His family was what we here in Texas call "salt of the earth" people—dependable and hardworking. In college Mark was swayed by humanism, and at the same time, life's disappointments caused him to doubt. He never really came to the point of denying the existence of God—in short, he was a picture of agnosticism.

Over the years Mark and I went through several periods where we found ourselves at odds with each other. (This is not the case at all now.) I determined that I needed to pray for him in a concerted fashion, and pray I did—for six long years.

During those years, I mixed the spiritual weapons of prayer and fasting—and then I would pray and fast some more. One year passed and then another and things did not seem to get any better. Mike and I would speak with Mark from time to time, but most often it did not end well. I am not saying it was his fault as a person; of course, we were not battling against flesh and blood. There were forces of darkness that were very afraid of Mark Reithmiller coming to Christ.

Lucy had her dramatic encounter with the Lord first, but with his background in science, Mark simply could not grasp that there really is a God and that His son is Jesus Christ. There was a very sweet side to the battle at this point, though—my sister was standing side by side with me in prayer for Mark.

The good thing is that God is well able to deal with tough cases like Mark. Some people seem to need a supernatural visitation from God completely outside of what can be grasped from a natural understanding—such was Mark's case.

One night, seemingly out of the blue, a voice awakened Mark. It was the same one that Saul heard on the road to Damascus. "Mark, I am the one you are resisting. I am God!" Mark's room lit up with a bright light and at that moment he knew that Jesus was the only way to heaven and that He was God.

Have you ever noticed that God can be rather dramatic at times? The funny thing is that my sister slept through the whole encounter. From that day, Mark gave his life to Jesus Christ and became a Christian.

One of the most powerful quotes about persistence in prayer that I have ever read is from George Müller, who said:

> The point is never to give up until the answer comes. I have been praying for sixty-three years and eight months for one man's conversion. He is not saved yet but he will be. How can it be otherwise . . . I am praying.

The day came when Müller's friend received Christ. It did not come until Müller's casket was lowered into the ground. There, near the open grave, this friend gave his heart to God. Prayers of perseverance had won another battle. Müller's success may be summarized in four powerful words: *He did not quit.*[5]

Chapter Five

Fasting

*I*n my late twenties, I became very hungry for God and started devouring Christian books that I felt would help me grow spiritually. One subject that was particularly interesting to me was fasting.

Fasting! I thought. *Does that mean they go completely without food?* By that time I had heard my pastor mention a Bible concordance, so I asked Mike to buy me one for my birthday. One of the first words I looked up was *fasting*. I read the Scripture references with deep interest. The one that leapt off the pages of the Bible above all others on this subject was Isaiah 58:6:

> Is this not the fast that I have chosen: to loose the bonds
> of wickedness, to undo the heavy burdens, to let the oppressed
> go free, and that you break every yoke?

After reading this and other Scriptures, I decided I needed to fast. So I did—*breakfast.* By ten o'clock my hands were shaking and

I felt weak. My body was mad at me and thought I was starving it. By eleven, I felt even worse and thought I might be dying. You have probably figured out by now that at noon I ate lunch.

Pondering my inglorious introduction to fasting, I made several really good decisions. First, I went and bought my first book on the subject, *God's Chosen Fast* by Arthur Wallis. I really didn't know what I was doing, but now I know the Lord was leading me to one of the best and most easily understood books on the subject. Second, I figured my body must be in bad shape if I could not fast more than one meal without shaking from head to toe! So next I went out and purchased some really good vitamins and started a healthy diet regimen.

After that I found another powerful verse related to fasting:

> But I discipline my body and bring it into subjection, lest, when I have preached to others, I myself should become disqualified.
>
> 1 CORINTHIANS 9:27

After my initial attempt at fasting, I recognized that winning the battle of my flesh and its desire for food over God, food definitely was the victor. In fact, since I had never once in my life abstained from eating in order to fast, my flesh won the first round. I now realized, however, that as a Christian I needed to *subject* my flesh or, as the *Revised Standard Version* says, *pommel* (or *pummel*) it to bring it under subjection to God. *Pummel* is a very strong word. A synonym is *buffet*. Of course, it's a given I am not speaking of a physical beating of one's own body.

This is the spiritual point that I want to make: One of the primary ways we as believers experience spiritual breakthrough and growth is through prayer mixed with fasting.

The Christian's Call to Fasting

Someone once asked me if I thought it was the Christian's duty to fast. My answer is yes. If you aren't able to abstain totally from food due to health issues or concerns, there are alternative ways to "pummel" and discipline your body to bring it under subjection. A physical body disciplined through fasting is a sign of a disciplined spiritual life.

Spiritual discipline in fasting is one of the basics of a Christian's life. As I look at the words I've just written, it shocks me to think that I didn't follow this important biblical discipline prior to my early thirties. Taking this thought one step further, I also know that many Christians either have not been taught to fast as a part of their spiritual life or have never taken the spiritual challenge from Scripture.

As I have studied the lives of many Christian leaders, it seems that each of those whom I consider to be my spiritual heroes fasted on a regular basis. The late Welsh prayer warrior Rees Howells is one of my "mentors from history" on intercessory prayer. Here is what he went through as he subjected his flesh to a time of fasting, according to author Norman Grubb:

> It was at a time when he had a great burden for a certain convention, which was being disrupted by assaults of the enemy. The Lord called him to a day of prayer and fasting, which was something new to him. Used to, as he was, a comfortable home and four good meals a day, it came as a shock to realize that it meant no dinner, and he was agitating about it. And would it only happen once? Supposing God asked him to do it every day!
>
> When midday came he was on his knees in his bedroom, but there was no prayer that next hour. "I didn't know there

was such a lust in me," he said afterwards. "My agitation was the proof of the grip it had on me. If the thing had no power over me, why did I argue about it?"

At one o'clock his mother called him, and he told her he wasn't taking lunch. But she called again, as a mother would, and urged, "It won't take you long to have it." The goodly aroma from downstairs was too much for him, and down he came. But, after the meal, when he returned to his room, he couldn't get back into the presence of God. He came face to face with disobedience to the Holy Ghost.

"I felt I was like the man in the Garden of Eden. I went up the mountain and walked miles, cursing the old man within me." . . . He didn't take dinner for many days after that, but spent the hour with God. As he said later, "The moment I got victory in it, it wasn't a very big thing to do. . . . It is while you still want a thing that you can't get your mind off it. When you have risen above it, He may give it back to you; but then you are out of it."[1]

Keeping yourself under personal discipline is important to the prayer life of an individual; not only does fasting bring spiritual breakthrough but it also serves to purify your life.

Fasting and Spiritual Purity

It is particularly sad to me to see spiritual leaders fall into sins of the flesh. It seems to me that there is often a direct correlation between the power over temptations such as sexual sin and a fasting life. When one controls the physical appetite, the authority gained through that spiritual disciple extends to power over other kinds of temptation as well.

As Christians, we need to learn to control our appetites so that we are not disqualified as witnesses for the work of the ministry. This ties in to the Scripture from 1 Corinthians 9:27, where the apostle Paul says he disciplines his body to bring it into subjection.

The point is this: Whatever rules over us in the physical realm more than God's will and Word has the potential to in some measure keep us from walking in God's highest and best.

One day I went to the kitchen to make my morning iced tea. I know that the thought of drinking an iced drink for breakfast may not have great appeal for some people, but remember that I am a Texan and iced tea is, for most of us, the cultural drink of choice. I drink it even if there is an ice storm outside. Right in the middle of my tea-making ritual, I heard the Lord say within me, "Cindy, you cannot let that iced tea rule you, nor the caffeine in it. Abstain for three days."

"Three days without iced tea? No problem!" I blithely shot back. I am a submitted woman of God, and no cool glass of the Texas state beverage was going to have a hold on me! Oh, but I was wrong—really wrong. By the end of the first day I wanted a glass of tea and it had to be cold. At the end of the second day I had a terrible headache and would have drunk it without ice. The third day I would have forced down tea bags, or swilled even very bad week-old tea!

Since that valuable lesson, I try to be sensitive to the Lord when my body needs to be put under submission. For instance, at times I've been called to specifically forgo things like chocolate, coffee, and even ice cream. One time Mike and I went on a thirty-five-day no-sweets or pleasant-drinks fast. I think that one was almost harder than no food at all. Mike's fast in that manner continued for two-plus years.

Certain kinds of food and beverage are like crutches in moments of stress. We sometimes call them "comfort food" here in Texas. It isn't bad for us to enjoy comfort food—we just can't let the appetite for it control us.

The Rewards of Fasting

I know by now some of you are wishing you had never read this chapter. Don't think that I am not feeling deeply for you as I write. In fact, at times the thought of fasting without my favorite dessert—Blue Bell ice cream—strikes deep into my comfort food zone. One time there was a fire in Brenham, Texas, where the Blue Bell creamery is located. And though it seems crass, the conversations I heard weren't filled with concern about the people of the town—everyone just wanted to know if the Blue Bell creamery had survived!

Sometimes when I know I am going to fast, I make a trip to my grocer's freezer section and grab a couple of half gallons of Blue Bell Homemade Vanilla. I return home, throw it in my freezer, and say, "I'll see you later." Yum! It is the best reward after fasting.

According to Isaiah 58:5, fasting is a day to afflict the soul. I have to agree with that statement. One day during a long fast, as I drove down the streets of my city, I said right out loud, "God, your Word is right! My soul is feeling really afflicted." Instead of feeling more spiritual, I was dreaming of food and thinking about not thinking about food.

Joking aside, there are spiritual rewards that come from fasting, and many of the mightiest spiritual leaders have made this discipline a big part of their lives. Fasting places you right up there with some great Christian leaders who are in God's Hall of Fame, such as the men in the famous Holy Club at Oxford University, started by the Wesley brothers, John and Charles.

The young men in the club were jeeringly called "Methodists" because they systematically tried to serve God every hour of the day. They served through philanthropy toward the poor, living on a set income no matter how their personal fortunes increased, celebrating Holy Communion frequently, and by fasting on Wednesdays and Fridays until 3:00 p.m.[2] Three of the most noted members of the Holy Club were John and Charles Wesley and George Whitefield.

When John Wesley ordained Francis Asbury as the first Methodist bishop to America, no Methodist minister was allowed to preach unless he fasted every week.[3]

I believe that God is going to use many young university students today to form such Holy Clubs with prayer and fasting as their focus as they intercede for their campuses.

Have I convinced you yet that you need to fast? There are certain answers to prayer that we will never see unless we combine prayer with fasting. Note that Jesus said, "*when* you fast," not "*if* you fast" (Matthew 6:16–17). Biblically, fasting is not something that is optional in the life of a Christian.

At times people come to me and say, "I have prayed and prayed but not seen the answer to my prayer." And I will say, "Have you fasted?" If they have and are not seeing the answer, then I say, "Well, fast and pray some more."

It's critical to remember that the powers of darkness war against our prayers in order to keep them from fulfillment. This was the case with Daniel:

> Then he (the angel) said to me, "Do not fear, Daniel, for from the first day that you set your heart to understand, and to humble yourself before your God, your words were heard; and I have come because of your words. But the prince of the kingdom of Persia withstood me twenty-one days; and behold,

Michael, one of the chief princes, came to help me, for I had been left alone there with the kings of Persia."

DANIEL 10:12–13

At the time of this angelic visitation, Daniel had fasted for three full weeks (Daniel 10:2–3). We also know that Daniel lived a life of discipline and abstinence because he, along with the three Hebrew princes, refused to eat the rich foods of Babylon. Oh, that a generation would arise who would dare to be a Daniel in society today! My prayer is for many young leaders to live a fasted life so they can be an influence in their own modern-day Babylon.

Some youth movements, such as The Call, have encouraged forty-day fasts where the students give away their lunches to another student who might be hungry. In recent years, a number of youth as young as thirteen years old have gone on extended fasts as they pray for America and for the ending of abortion. My son, Daniel, has done a number of annual fasts where he eats only vegetables for twenty-one days in order to walk in his destiny as a Daniel.

Pursuing the Fasted Life

In addition to fasting in order to "pummel" the body and keep it well-tuned spiritually, there are many other blessings that come from fasting. I recommend that every believer live the fasted life, where one fasts on a regular basis as a spiritual discipline. This is what the members of the Holy Club did as a matter of course. As you enter into the fasted life, you will keep yourself at a spiritual optimum, proactively able to deal with life's crises, rather than always being on your heels emotionally and spiritually. When a crisis does occur, it will not be as hard for you to add more time of fasting to your weekly discipline.

The curative power of living a fasted life is purported by many people who work in the field of nutrition. Plutarch, the famous Greek philosopher and biographer (circa AD 46–120), said: "Instead of using medicine, fast a day."

In recent years there has been considerable investigation into Plutarch's branch of natural therapy by qualified experts in Europe, the U.S., and Britain, and remarkable results have been achieved in clinics where "the healing fast" (as it is sometimes called) is practiced.[4]

Fasting in Concert With Others

During various seasons of life, Mike and I have entered into covenantal Wednesday morning fasts where we focus in prayer on each of our children. At other times we have joined with other groups to fast and pray for our nation on the first Friday of the month.

I love this kind of fasting in concert, as it multiplies the strength of the fast by the number of people fasting. In addition, there is a knitting together of hearts and purpose that is a special added joy. A number of churches I am acquainted with, including my own, Trinity Church of Cedar Hill, Texas, begin the year with a fast. We have seen many wonderful breakthroughs through corporate fasting.

Louisville, Kentucky, pastor Bob Rodgers, whose church begins each New Year with a twenty-one-day fast, highlights the benefits of a corporate fast:

1. Fasting with others gives you the incentive not to break the fast prematurely. Pastor Bob suggests that this follows the old adage: Misery loves company.

2. Fasting in January and February each year brings unity in families and helps avert the domestic violence and family breakups prevalent during these two months. It also mitigates against church splits that often take place during this time period.

3. Fasting gives corporate breakthroughs. When one person in the group receives a breakthrough, the whole group receives it along with him.[5]

I also love the fact that Bob and his church ask for congregation-wide breakthroughs in the following ways:

- Permanent weight loss from the fast
- A 25 percent increase in income that year
- Prodigals returning to the Lord
- Household salvations
- Healings of incurable diseases

The most common length of a shorter fast is three days. Many people believe this is the most helpful for them to see spiritual breakthroughs, rather than a long fast.

It is my personal belief that at least once in our lives, we should go on a much longer fast of some sort—either a twenty-one-day or a forty-day fast. This kind of fast is usually, but not always, a "called" fast. By this I mean that you are fasting out of a clear conviction and calling from the Lord. In such a case, you will receive special grace from Him to sustain you during that time. And as mentioned earlier, there are many types of long fasts (e.g., a no-sweets fast, a Daniel fast [only vegetables], etc.).

Fasting Wisely and Healthily

Before you embark on any fast, it is important to use wisdom and caution. For example, an expectant mother should not fast, as her body is providing essential nutrients to the child growing within her. Other people with medical conditions, such as diabetes, can ask God what kind of fast they can undertake that enters into the spiritual discipline without endangering their health and life. It is wise and prudent to consult your physician if you have questions or doubts about what your body can handle. Be assured, however, that God will not call you to fast if it is going to damage your health or metabolism. I personally have friends who went on so many forty-day fasts that their bodies kicked into "starvation mode" and they had trouble losing weight from then on.

Since it is my conviction that at least one long fast of some kind greatly deepens a person's spiritual walk, it is important to know how to fast responsibly. Put simply, God doesn't want us to damage our physical temples. Along this same line, because of my travel schedule, I will often use protein drinks in the morning when on a liquid fast to keep up my physical stamina.

Fasting is a spiritual exercise and can be likened to physical exertion. Just as a person needs to gradually build up their muscular strength, so they should do the same in preparation for a fast. Maybe you are like I was in my early twenties, when I had never fasted before. Remember that my body protested loudly after missing just one meal! Begin with baby steps—starting with a one-meal or one-day fast, and then, as the Lord leads, build up to a longer fast. In His grace, I do not believe God would call a person to a forty-day fast, as a rule, if they have never fasted a day in their life!

When Daniel was taken captive into Babylon, he refused to eat the king's delicacies and drink the royal wine. There are a number of possible reasons why Daniel chose not to partake of the Babylonian foods he encountered. Two could have been that the foods offered were not prepared in a kosher fashion, or that the meat had been sacrificed or dedicated to Babylonian idols.

Regardless of the reason for Daniel's abstinence, this self-discipline prepared him for the long fasts that he would do later on in his life. In Daniel 9:3, we see where Daniel fasted and mourned in intercession for the sins of his people so they could be released from captivity. Then Daniel 10:2–3 tells us that he fasted three full weeks without pleasant food, meat, or wine. His ability to fast and pray for a longer period of time was evident, and it resulted in spiritual breakthrough into the wisdom and understanding he was seeking.

Note the wisdom God used (1 Kings 17:1–16) in sending the prophet Elijah to a widow for a simple diet of bread and oil after being sustained by bits of food brought to him by ravens. The Lord could have sent him to a king's palace if He had wanted to!

Preparing for a Fast

1. Begin to curtail your eating. Eat simple meals and smaller amounts of food. This will prepare your body and start to shrink your stomach.

2. Start cutting back on the liquids from which you are going to abstain, such as caffeine drinks (coffee, tea, or soda). This will help you avoid the not-so-fun second-day headaches.

3. Seek the Lord for the kind of fast you are to pursue (e.g., partial, such as vegetables [Daniel fast], or full fast [water or juice only]).

4. Ask the Lord about the length of the fast.

5. Determine the reason you are fasting (for whom or what are you praying?).

6. Make a list of the things you want to see happen during your time of fasting.

Breaking a Fast

It is extremely important to break a fast gradually. I personally know people who became quite ill after eating a normal diet immediately after a long fast. One friend ate a complete Chinese dinner after a forty-day fast and ended up in the emergency room! In addition, I have heard stories of people who actually died from going back to eating a full diet after an extended period of fasting.

Here are some ways that I personally break a long fast:

1. After a fast of three or more days, I begin with clear soup or some kind of soft soup for the first meal.

2. If my system seems to handle that well, at the next meal I move up to soft vegetables, such as mashed potatoes or green cooked vegetables.

3. Usually by the second or third day, I can move on to

a meal with some kind of meat, while still leaving out spicy foods.

Benefits of Fasting

There are many benefits to fasting found in Scripture; therefore, the following list is not meant to be exhaustive. I quoted earlier from Bob Rodgers' book *101 Reasons to Fast*. Below are six of his reasons to fast. Obviously my selections include those that I consider key to prayer and fasting breakthroughs. I have added my comments after the points.

1. REMOVE SPIRITUAL OBSTACLES

There are times when we are in prayer and nothing seems to be changing the current situation. For instance, when we are facing a mountain of debt or are grappling with other large obstacles. When our prayers are not breaking through, we need to add fasting to the mix, just as Jesus instructed His disciples in Matthew 17:20–21:

> Jesus said to them, "Because of your unbelief, for assuredly, I say to you, if you have faith as a mustard seed, you will say to this mountain, 'Move from here to there,' and it will move; and nothing will be impossible for you. However, this kind does not go out except by prayer and fasting."

2. NEED OF HEALING

Fasting is a biblical means of receiving healing, as highlighted in Isaiah 58:8: "Then your light shall break forth like the morning, your healing shall spring forth speedily."

3. When faced with calamity

For instance, if you are in the midst of an economic crisis of huge proportions or are the victim of some natural calamity.

4. To hear the voice of the Holy Spirit

The Holy Spirit spoke to the prophets and teachers in Antioch while they fasted and prayed that they should separate Paul and Barnabas unto the ministry (Acts 13:1–3).

5. In order to have provision for the poor

Fasting is very important when one has a calling to social justice issues, such as feeding the poor. As a starting point, those with this type of calling can fast and give away the money they would have otherwise spent on food (Isaiah 58:7).

6. Fasting for a national awakening and reformation

There are times in the history of a nation when moral decline and degradation is so great that a supernatural miracle is needed to stop the slide into judgment. Many nations of the world, such as the United States, are in need of an awakening and reformation. While many are fasting and praying for the U.S., we still need more intercession to see the nation break through to righteousness. It is part of our role as Christians to stand in the gap for our nations through prayer and fasting.

The prophet Joel speaks powerfully of this call for fasting and prayer to bring about repentance for individuals and nations:

"Now, therefore," says the Lord, "Turn to Me with all your heart, with fasting, with weeping, and with mourning." Blow the trumpet in Zion, consecrate a fast.

JOEL 2:12, 15

Prayer and Fasting for a Nation

A number of United States presidents have understood their role as national leaders to call for fasting and prayer on behalf of the nation. They recognized the need to seek the mercies of the living God. One such president was Abraham Lincoln, who issued the following proclamation, requested by the Senate during the Civil War:

> *Whereas, the Senate of the United States devoutly recognizes the Supreme Authority and Just Government of Almighty God, in all the affairs of men and of nations, has, by a resolution, requested the President to designate and set apart a day for National Prayer and Humiliation [Fasting].*
>
> *And whereas, it is the duty of nations, as well as of men, to own their dependence upon the overruling power of God, to confess their sins and transgressions, in humble sorrow, yet with assured hope that genuine repentance will lead to mercy and pardon; and to recognize the sublime truth, announced in the Holy Scriptures and proven by all history, that those nations only are blessed whose God is the Lord. . . .*
>
> *All this being done, in sincerity and truth, let us then rest humbly in the hope authorized by the Divine teachings, that the united cry of the Nation will be heard on high, and answered with blessings, no less than the pardon of our national sins, and restoration of our now divided and suffering country, to its former happy condition of unity and peace.*[6]

Historically, other United States leaders have understood the need to personally fast and pray for the nation. George Washington fasted when called upon to do so by the House of Burgesses in Virginia. His personal diary reads: *"Went to church and fasted all day." June 1, 1774*[7]

The Lord is longing to find such godly leaders among the nations today: men and women who will call their people to prayer and repentance. I believe there are many Daniels, Josephs, Esthers, and Deborahs whom God is calling today to run for public office who will one day again issue such proclamations.

In closing this chapter, I want to stress that it is not meant to be a complete guide to fasting, but rather a starting point to increase your prayer life by combining it with fasting. If you are interested in delving further, there are many good books on fasting, including Elmer L. Towns, *Fasting for Spiritual Breakthrough* (Regal Books, 1995).

The spiritual discipline of fasting is one of the most important and powerful weapons in our spiritual arsenal, and in the next chapter we will learn how to pray the Word of God. With these dynamic tools there is nothing in heaven or on earth that will be able to withstand God's will from being accomplished in our lives.

Chapter Six

Praying the Word

*M*any years ago on a beautiful California morning, my left-brained, cerebral husband awakened me with the pronouncement, "Cindy, we are going to have a son and we are to call him Daniel!" He then proceeded to relate how he had a dream in which God had shown him we were going to have a son.

I have to admit that at that moment I stared at my husband with a look of shock as I pondered in my heart what he had just said to me. My next very unspiritual thought was: *An alien has stolen my husband's body!* You see, I am the dreamer and musician, and Mike is the business-minded, numbers-crunching kind of guy. Later on we could see God's wisdom in speaking to Mike.

When Daniel was born we had quite a battle for his life. It was a very difficult time fraught with complications, and fear would sometimes grip my heart as the enemy would try to tell me that Daniel would not live. Daniel was—and is—a born fighter, and live he did!

Then after several months, I started noticing that he seemed to be lagging behind in some areas of normal development. First of all, he could not pull himself up in his crib. Daniel had been born with a clubfoot, and it was placed in a cast to help correct the problem. Of course we were doing everything we could to help him be 100 percent in every way.

When Daniel was ten months old, however, our pediatrician said the words that no parent wants to hear: "Mrs. Jacobs, there seems to be something wrong with the muscle tone in your son's leg." I watched in shock as the doctor tapped Daniel's leg with the little rubber instrument that tests muscular reflexes—Daniel had none. There was simply no reflex response. With a look of concern, the doctor gently repeated the test. Still nothing. I knew then that my suspicions had been correct—there was something very wrong with Daniel's leg.

The prognosis was not good; without muscle tone Daniel might never walk. I went home from the doctor with our four-year-old daughter in tow and Daniel in my arms. What were we going to do? Mike had recently landed a job in Dallas, and the children and I were still in El Paso, Texas, waiting for our house to sell.

That night I opened my Bible to read and a Scripture seemed to leap off the page:

> But those who wait for the Lord [who expect, look for, and hope in Him] shall change and renew their strength and power; they shall lift their wings and mount up [close to God] as eagles [mount up to the sun]; they shall run and not be weary; they shall walk and not faint or become tired.
>
> ISAIAH 40:31 AMP

I knew God gave that Scripture to me for that exact moment in time. My son was meant to walk—and run! It was as though

God had given Mike and me something to hang on to in order to believe in and claim Daniel's healing.

The Power of Praying God's Word

From then on, at every diaper change I would pray for Daniel's leg and foot, and say out loud, "Daniel, you are going to run and not be weary and walk and not faint. Son, one day you are going to stand up and walk!"

I would like to be able to write that the first time I quoted that Scripture over Daniel he suddenly stood up and walked, but it didn't happen that way. As I mentioned, we first received the report when Daniel was ten months old and we were living in El Paso.

Two months later our El Paso home sold and we moved to Weatherford, Texas. Daniel's first birthday came and went, and he still couldn't stand on his own or pull himself up. I kept quoting Isaiah 40:31 over him, and little by little he started improving. One day when Mike's mom was holding him, he pulled up and stood. However, he still could not maintain balance and walk.

The months passed by until Daniel was almost seventeen months old. One Wednesday night we were in church. Out of the corner of my eye, I saw something small trundling down the center aisle of the church, and sure enough, it was our little Daniel. He was walking completely on his own, and not holding on to anything. Plus, he had a big smile on his face.

Praying the Word works!

During the time that I was standing upon the promise of Isaiah 40:31 for Daniel's healing, I also came across a book by Germaine Copeland entitled *Prayers That Avail Much* (Harrison House). The book was made up of prayers, containing Scriptures that could be used for various categories of needs. What I read about praying the Word impacted me so greatly that I started planting Scripture deeply into each prayer, with amazing results. I once heard someone say that the Word works for those who work the Word.

As I started writing this chapter, I wondered if there was a story behind Germaine's writing *Prayers That Avail Much*? Since reading her book nearly thirty years ago, Germaine and I have become dear friends, so I called her up to ask her.

I could tell she was smiling when she answered my question. "Why, yes," she said, "I started studying about praying the Word during a very difficult time with my son, David."

Here is her story gleaned from our conversation:

"In the early '70s I discovered that our son was into drugs. This drove me to study the subject of prayer in the Bible. One particular Scripture that stood out to me was James 5:16b: 'The effectual fervent prayer of a righteous man availeth much' " (KJV).

Germaine went on to explain that if some prayers were effectual, then she reasoned some were ineffectual. Of course, she was interested in praying effective prayers because she had a big problem: a son in deep trouble! She needed prayers that would avail much. Perfectly logical, right?

It has been said that today's tests are tomorrow's testimonies, and that life's deepest valleys are the roadways to God's greatest glory. This was certainly the case with Germaine Copeland. Rather than letting the sorrow of her son's addiction overcome her, she used the problem to drive her to the most powerful prayer tool in the world—praying the Word of God.

Each time she would hear something else that her prodigal son was doing, she would open her Bible and claim God's promises. At last she started writing out her prayers and filling them full of Scripture. One of her favorites was—and still is—1 John 5:14–15:

> Now this is the confidence that we have in Him, that if we ask anything according to His will, He hears us. And if we know that He hears us, whatever we ask, we know that we have the petition that we have asked of Him.

This praying mother had to stand on God's Word and learn to never let go, even in the midst of circumstances that seemed to go from bad to worse. It seems that her boy would get better for a while and then turn back to his old ways. One terrible day she received the message that the object of her intercession, David, had been arrested.

Germaine went to her prayer closet to talk to God about this problem, and He spoke to her, "I had him arrested." After that, she didn't worry about David while he was in prison. She figured that if God arrested David, then He would take care of him even while he was incarcerated. At the point of his arrest, Germaine had been praying for her son for twenty-eight years.

God had tried to get David's attention on many occasions—before finally slamming a prison door in his face. Three times before, David had known God was telling him he had to stop using drugs. But David had not listened, and always responded, "I'll stop when I finish this cocaine." Of course he never did.

At last, locked away in a prison cell where he had to face his addictions, David began to understand that God had put him behind bars as a way of escape from the life he led. God spoke in an audible voice and told him that he had to choose life or death. The fear of the Lord gripped David, and he knew without a doubt that he would die if he didn't change. He also knows today that if he had died then, he would have gone to hell. David surrendered his life completely to the Lord and was dramatically and forever changed.

After that time, David started studying the Scriptures and sought to mend and rebuild the broken relationships in his life. He took personal responsibility for his actions rather than always blaming others for his problems. All of this took place ten years before my interview with Germaine, and I am happy to say that David now works in his mother's prayer ministry. He also faithfully attends an accountability growth group entitled Victorious Living.

Much fruit has come from Germaine's fighting the good fight of faith for twenty-eight years. During those years of trial, she went on to write her classic series of Scripture prayer books entitled *Prayers That Avail Much*.

I asked Germaine how many books have sold to date from that series.

She replied with a sweet chuckle in her voice, "Over four million."

Now that is what I call effectual prayer! Germaine's persistence in prayer reminds me of a wonderful verse:

> For our light affliction, which is but for a moment, is working for us a far more exceeding and eternal weight of glory.
>
> 2 CORINTHIANS 4:17

Some of you reading this chapter are going through a difficult time right now. Be assured that one day God is going to turn your situation into an eternal weight of glory. Your test will become a testimony from which you will be able to comfort others.

Steps for Praying God's Word

How does one get started praying the Word? First of all, you need to realize that God uses the Scriptures to facilitate the supernatural. The verses you are going to stand on in prayer are not words simply written by man but are inspired by the Holy Spirit. When prayed and believed, these promises have the power to change even the darkest circumstances. God's Word is living and powerful (Hebrews 4:12)!

Here is one example of standing on the Word in prayer: Let's say you are in the midst of an unjust situation and it seems your life is falling apart. This would be a great opportunity to pray and stand on Romans 8:28:

> We are assured and know that [God being a partner in their labor] all things work together and are [fitting into a plan] for good to and for those who love God and are called according to [His] design and purpose.
>
> AMP

After I find a verse like this, I will often write the day's date in the margin of my Bible. You may not be comfortable writing in your Bible, but I love to write notes in the margins and put dates and even places where I have prayed. For me, this is like writing a book of remembrance. Later I can read what I wrote and rejoice in and be strengthened by the Lord's answers.

Sometimes when I get up in the night to pray and am wrestling over a certain issue in intercession, I will leaf through the pages of my Bible and read those notes. Some were written while ministering in other nations. The book of Isaiah (my favorite) is particularly marked with margin notes penned in

Iraq, Kuwait, Turkey, England, Argentina, Costa Rica, Spain, and other places.

I've often thought that someday my grandchildren and their children might look at those same notes and hear the voice of God through the Scriptures I have claimed in prayer.

Earlier I mentioned that you might want to write a Scripture prayer if you are involved in an unjust situation (or you can use the sample one given here):

> *Father God, I thank you that your Word says all things in my life will work for good because I am fulfilling the purpose that you have set out for me. Therefore, I believe this situation I am in now will turn out for my good. It is impossible for it to turn out any other way. I thank you and praise you, Father, that even now circumstances are being worked out for my future that are being turned around in ways beyond what I can imagine or dream. In Jesus' name. Amen.*

For a court case, you might add this:

> *Father God, I thank you that because I walk uprightly before you and trust you, I find favor with both God and man. Therefore, I declare that I have favor before the judges of the earth.*

The more we learn God's Word, the easier it will become to claim Scriptures in prayer and combine them in effective ways that will avail much on our behalf.

Adding more verses to your prayers strengthens the anointing upon them and adds richness to your intercession. You will soon learn to use Scripture-based prayer as a "sword of the spirit" (Hebrews 4:12) to cut off spiritual darkness and to open the way for God's power to move in a situation or for the person for whom you are interceding.

Here is another great verse to use as an opening to your prayers:

> For the eyes of the Lord are upon the righteous (those who are upright and in right standing with God), and His ears are attentive to their prayer.
>
> 1 PETER 3:12 AMP

As a starting place in your journey of praying God's Word, I suggest you write out your prayers in a journal and then read them out loud.

Using 1 Peter 3:12, you could open your prayer with the following:

> Father God, I thank you that your eyes are upon me today as I pray and that your ears are attentive and open to my prayers. I believe that you hear me.

In Germaine Copeland's book series *Prayers That Avail Much*, she has written a collection of prayers to be used for intercession. Here is one for use in interceding for your children:

> *Father, in the name of Jesus, I pray and confess Your Word over my children and surround them with my faith—faith in Your Word that You watch over it to perform it! I confess and believe that my children are disciples of Christ, taught of the Lord and obedient to Your will. Great is the peace and undisturbed composure of my children, because You, God, contend with that which contends with my children, and You give them safety and ease them.*
>
> *Father, You will perfect that which concerns me. I commit and cast the care of my children once and for all over on You, Father. They are in Your hands, and I am positively persuaded that You are able to guard and keep that which I have committed to You. You are more than enough!*

I confess that my children obey their parents in the Lord as His repre-
sentatives, because this is just and right. My children _____
honor, esteem, and value as precious their parents; for this is the first
commandment with promise: that all may be well with my children
and that they may live long on the earth. I believe and confess that my
children choose life and love You, Lord, obey Your voice and cling to You;
for You are their Life and length of their days. Therefore, my children are
the head and not the tail, and they shall be above only and not beneath.
They are blessed when they come in and when they go out.

As parents, we will not provoke, irritate, or fret our children. We
will not be hard on them or harass them or cause them to become dis-
couraged, sullen, or morose, or to feel inferior and frustrated. We will
not break or wound their spirits, but will rear them in the admonition
of the Lord. We will train them in the way they should go, and when
they are old, they will not depart from it.

O Lord, my Lord, how excellent (majestic and glorious) is Your
Name in all the earth! You have set Your glory on or above the heavens.
Out of the mouths of babes and unweaned infants You have established
strength because of Your foes, that You might silence the enemy and
the avenger. I sing praises to Your name, O Most High. The enemy is
turned back from my children in the name of Jesus! They increase in
wisdom and in favor with God and man. Amen.[1]

Some people might want to buy a new journal each year
and write their prayers for the year in them as their own book
of remembrance. Others, like me, might prefer to write in the
margins of their Bible. I can always tell when a person has learned
to pray the Word as I listen to them pray aloud. Their prayers
will be rich, deep, and effective.

Historically, various denominations have sanctioned prayer
books for various seasons of the year or sacramental functions
using such passages as the Lord's Prayer. Last year, when I went
home to visit my mom, I found a tiny white book at her house.
Opening the pages, I read the flyleaf: *The Book of Common Prayer*
and Administration of the Sacraments and Other Rites and Ceremonies

of the Church. According to the use of the Protestant Episcopal Church in the United States of America. (New York: Thomas Nelson and Sons, 1944).

"What's this, Mom?" I asked.

"Honey, I carried that book when Dad and I got married." After she said that, I checked the front page:

> *In the Name of the Father, and of the Son, and of the Holy Ghost. Amen.*
>
> *This certifies that* **Eleanor McJilton** *and* **Albert S. Johnson** *were united in Holy Matrimony on May 24ᵗʰ, 1944, in Oak Cliff Presbyterian Church, Dallas, Texas.*

Being raised Baptist, I didn't even know there was a *Book of Common Prayer*, so I read some of the history of it. I found that it has been through various edits and even times of great controversy. During dark times, however, it was a book used to keep prayer alive in the church, and people were able to pray the prayer of agreement by using it. As I looked over the written prayers, I realized that they were full of Scripture. While many people may not have been raised with liturgical-style prayer, I believe there is a place for this ancient practice in the body of Christ.

Praying God's Word in Concert With Others

One vital aspect of praying the Word is the act of congregations praying together. We need to refresh our focus not only on adults praying together but also Scripture-based prayer that involves every age group. Wouldn't it be wonderful if whole churches prayed the Word over the children in their congregations?

The Word of God is living and powerful and sharper than any two-edged sword (Hebrews 4:12)! We need to learn to wield it effectually in fervent intercession to see not only our households saved but whole cities! Imagine scores of cities adopting prayers from the Word as their very own.

As I mentioned in an earlier chapter, various United States presidents have called for times of prayer and written proclamations urging the nation to cry out to God together. Keying off of President Lincoln's proclamation for a day of prayer and fasting, I wrote the following adaptation to call the United States to pray in 2010:

Proclamation of a Year of Repentance:

Whereas, the Senate of the United States of America has aforetimes issued National Proclamations of Prayer and Fasting, where it devoutly recognized the Supreme Authority and Just Government of Almighty God in all the affairs of men and of nations; we, the united believers in the Lord Jesus Christ, do declare and decree that we are one nation under God.

And, whereas, following the example and precedent of President Abraham Lincoln before us, we concur that it is the duty of nations, as well as of men, to own our dependence upon the overruling power of God and, as a people, confess our sins and transgressions against the most Holy God, and recognize the sublime truth, announced in the Holy Scriptures, that those nations only are blessed whose God is the Lord.

And, insomuch as we know that, by His divine law, nations, like individuals, are subjected to punishments and chastisements in this world, may we not fear that we are justly deserving of punishment for our presumptuous sins to the needful end of our national reformation as a whole People. We have been recipients of the choicest bounties of Heaven. We have been preserved, these many years, in peace and prosperity. We have grown in numbers, wealth, and power, as no other nation has ever grown; but we have forgotten God. We have forgotten the gracious hand which has preserved us in Peace, and multiplied and enriched and strengthened us; and we have vainly imagined, in the deceitfulness of our hearts, that all these blessings were produced by some superior wisdom and virtue of our own. Intoxicated with unbroken success, we have become too self-sufficient to feel the necessity of a redeeming and preserving grace, too proud to pray to the God that made us!

We have committed the sin of abortion, thus killing at least fifty-four million unborn children. We have committed the sin of buying and selling other human beings for our own self-serving purposes and greed. We have bowed at the altar of humanism and condoned effacing Your Name, God, from our nation's textbooks and schoolrooms. We have sinned against You and the nations of the world through the making of films that have glorified what is sinful and shameful in Your eyes. We have called good evil and evil good. All these things we have done and transgressed against Your Holy Name.

Therefore, it behooves us to humble ourselves before the offended Power, to confess our national sins, and to pray for clemency and forgiveness. We, as Christian leaders in the body of Christ in the United States of America, do call for a year of humility, fasting, and prayer to turn the nation back to God.

We do this in sincerity and truth with the hope authorized by the Divine teachings that the united cry of the believers of this Nation will be heard on High and answered with blessings and the restoration of our now economically and morally divided nation. We cry out for no less than the pardon of our national sins and the restoration of our land back to its former state as one Nation under God, the Lord Jesus Christ. We pray You will have mercy upon us, Lord, as believers who are crying under the imminent threat of religious persecution. We beseech You, Lord, to grant us elected leaders whose hearts are after You to return our nation to the vision our forefathers had when they fled religious persecution to establish a new dwelling place for freedom and the United States of America as a city set upon a hill, a beacon of light and freedom for all.

—CINDY JACOBS
ADAPTED FROM LINCOLN'S PROCLAMATION[2]

Such a presidential proclamation could be used as a prayer for the nation. My hope is that the nations of the world will be spurred to such public declarations in these difficult days.

The great U.S. Civil War-era minister E. M. Bounds (1835–1913), said this about prayer:

> Just as God commanded us to pray always, to pray everywhere, and to pray in everything, so He will answer always, everywhere, and in everything. God has plainly and with directness committed Himself to answered prayer. If we fulfill the conditions of prayer, the answer is bound to come. . . . The ordinances of nature might fail, but the ordinances of grace can never fail. There are no limitations, no adverse conditions, no weaknesses, and no inability that can or will hinder the answer to prayer. God's doing for us when we pray has no limitations and is not hedged about by provisos in Him or in the peculiar circumstances of any particular case. If we really pray, God masters and defies all things and is above all conditions.
>
> God explicitly says, "Call to Me, and I will answer you" (Jeremiah 33:3). There are no limitations, no hedges, and no hindrances in the way of God fulfilling the promise. His Word is at stake. His Word is involved. The God who cannot lie (Titus 1:2) is bound to answer. He has voluntarily placed himself under obligation to answer the prayer of those who truly pray.[3]

Praying the Word is the most powerful weapon we have in our prayer arsenal. Use it on a daily basis and you will see great answers in every circumstance of life, and your prayers will avail much.

Chapter Seven

Persistent Praise

*Y*ears ago Mike was laid off from his job with Trans World Airlines (TWA). We were young, had just bought our first house, and had a child to support. Things looked rather bleak. We had decided to get in our little Datsun and drive to Phoenix from Los Angeles for Christmas. The drive went from bad to worse as we had car trouble along the way.

At last we started for home, bundled up and sent off with the prayers of our family. As the day went on I pondered our future. What were we going back to? How were we going to live? Where was Mike going to work? All these questions swirled around in my brain.

All of a sudden I had the inspiration that we should praise God all the way home—and we did. We thanked Him for His provision, love, and mercy, and for our salvation. It was a supernatural praise meeting. We drove mile after mile into the darkening night and still the praises rolled out of our spirits. As soon as I would start to lag a bit, Mike would jump in and start singing.

And when he would flag low, words of thanksgiving would pop out of my mouth! There were moments when we would sing together. (Mike and I sang publicly in those days.)

After hours of this, we arrived home to our little white house in Los Angeles. In the natural, everything seemed the same. Mike had no job and our money was low, but we were rich in spiritual blessings.

Then the day after New Year's we received a phone call from the general manager of American Airlines in El Paso, Texas. Would Mike come out for an interview immediately? He flew out right away and went to work within a few weeks.

What happened? We were not aware that our praises were actually intercessory prayers at the time. Mike had been looking for jobs with no success and we were certainly being resisted in ways beyond natural reasoning. When we praised God together, Psalm 149:3–4 went into effect:

> Let them praise His name in chorus and choir and with the [single or group] dance let them sing praises to him with the tambourine and lyre! For the Lord takes pleasure in His people; He will beautify the humble with salvation and adorn the wretched with victory.
>
> AMP

God adorned us with victory after we praised Him, and it was a beautiful gift, indeed!

The Marriage of Praise and Prayer

Why include a chapter entitled "Persistent Praise" in a book about prayer? Years ago during a prayer time, the Lord spoke to my heart that prayer was praise and praise was prayer. At the time I didn't have a theological grid to back up what I thought I had heard. Later on, in 1986, Mike and I sponsored a meeting in Washington, D.C., called the Marriage of Prayer and Praise.

The fact that praise is intercessory is not such a surprising concept to many in the body of Christ today; but at the time it was a real revelation. I wrote about this time in my book *Possessing the Gates of the Enemy.*

During the Marriage of Prayer and Praise meeting, we had worship leader and songwriter Jim Gilbert stand up and share that intercessory praise can be found in Isaiah 56:7: "My house shall be called a house of prayer." Jim pointed out that the verse is actually referring to an intercessory song.

This was the key. I went home excited to study the verse further, and found that the words "of prayer," or *tephillah,* in Isaiah 56:7, can connote a prayer that is set to music and sung in formal worship. To my amazement and delight, I found that the word *tephillah* occurs seventy-seven times in the Old Testament.

You could safely interpret the verse this way: "My house shall be called a house of prayer and praise." Music cannot be separated from prayer in most of the Old Testament.[1]

In his book *Songs from Heaven,* Tommy Walker relates how the act of singing a new song to the Lord is really nothing more than praying: "During a worship concert, a woman shouted after the second song, 'You forgot to pray!' and I responded, 'Ma'am, that's what we've been doing.' The good news is that everyone can pray, which means that everyone can sing a new song to the Lord. For some of you, the melody may be only two or three notes, but if that melody is sung from your heart, it is a beautiful sound to your heavenly father."[2]

Worship doesn't usually come naturally in the midst of a tough situation. In fact, I find that it can be more of a discipline during tough, dry seasons. Once I really begin to focus on worshiping God more than on my current situation, the heaviness I am feeling seems to simply drop off.

When we hear bad news, many times our first response is fear. This was the case in 2 Chronicles 20, when Jehoshaphat was told about the vast Syrian army sent against the people of God.

Have you ever noticed that Satan seems to either send an overwhelming force of trouble against you or else tells you he has a great horde able to defeat you? Then he sends demonic forces of fear against you to enforce his victory.

I'm sure Jehoshaphat faced this challenge when considering the Syrians! However, he knew what to do when he was afraid: He set himself to seek the Lord and proclaimed a fast (2 Chronicles 20:3). He asked God to help them, and the Lord told the people through a prophet that they were not to be afraid. Then God spoke to them prophetically: "Position yourselves, stand still and see the salvation of the Lord!" (v. 17).

What position did they take? They bowed with their faces before God and worshiped. They didn't run around trying to find out how many swords or spears they had; they worshiped first.

Praise and Prayer as Spiritual Weapons

Persistent praise and worship in the face of great oppression causes great prayer victories. Many people stop worshiping when they get a good look at the enemy or face a big mountain of adversity. This is not the time to stop—it is the time to start!

I love what the Levites of the Kohathites and their children did in this serious circumstance—they stood up and praised God! Does that seem strange to you? Funny, but I don't think they teach that principle of battle in most war colleges today.

Then on the day of the battle itself, they believed the word of the Lord that had been given to them by the prophet Jahaziel and appointed singers to go before them in battle. I have often pictured this scene in my mind. The singers were faith-filled people; they were persistent in worship, particularly in the face of impossible odds. Normally one would think singers (if any) would stand *behind* the front-line infantry, but to them worship was first and foremost!

The Bible says that when they began to sing and praise the Lord, God set ambushes against the people of Ammon, Moab, and Mount Seir, who had come against Judah; and they were defeated.

This reminds me of another section of Psalm 149 that I wrote about earlier in the chapter:

> Let the high praises of God be in their mouth, and a two-edged sword in their hand, to execute vengeance on the nations, and punishments on the peoples; to bind their kings with chains, and their nobles with fetters of iron; to execute on them the written judgment—this honor have all His saints. Praise the Lord!
>
> PSALM 149:6–9

I like to imagine what happened as God's people worshiped. Most likely some very large angels went out and did battle on their behalf and stirred up trouble among the armies (the Lord set ambushes against them), because they turned against each other (2 Chronicles 20:21–23). What a brilliant battle strategy! After this time it wasn't God's people who were afraid anymore but their enemies!

Let's go over the progression that took place:

1. The enemy mounted against them with impossible odds.
2. God's people had to fight fear with praise.

3. They worshiped the Lord as a weapon of war.

4. Their enemies turned against themselves.

5. All the peoples were afraid of the great might of Judah.

All this happened because they chose to worship rather than retreat; they faced their fear and their enemies with persistent praise. Whenever you are faced with impossible odds, trust God that your persistent praise will lead you to victory.

In their book *The Worship Warrior*, Chuck Pierce and John Dickson talk about the power to overcome that is released when we magnify God. They point out that God has prepared a table before us in the presence of our enemies (Psalm 23:5).[3] Put another way, by faith we can actually taste the goodness of God when we worship, before it takes place.

The following is a great example of intercessory praise using the principle of praying the Word (explained in the last chapter). Try singing something like this aloud:

> Father God, I thank you and praise you that you are preparing a table for me in the presence of my enemies. Therefore, I do not have to be afraid of lack of any sort, because there is no lack in the kingdom of God. Your children are never forsaken nor their seed seen begging bread! I (my family) have adequate provision for every need. The enemies of fear and debt have no place in my (our) household. In Jesus' name. Amen. (Based on Psalms 23:5; 37:25.)

I particularly like to pray my Scripture prayers aloud; it is powerful when you turn them into a song. Faith comes by hearing, and hearing by the Word of God!

Imagine the faith that came when young Mary sang what is known as "The Magnificat." When we sing words like "Magnify the Lord," He is magnified and our situation is put into kingdom perspective! Our worship releases His power in an intercessory way that becomes more powerful than what Satan attempts to do in our lives.

Persistent Praise in Times of Difficulty

Not long ago I was reading my Bible and came across the passage that tells us to "rejoice in the Lord always." The passage goes on to say that we are to let our gentleness be known to all men (Philippians 4:4–5). Then I read Ephesians 5:20, which says to give thanks always for all things to God the Father in the name of our Lord Jesus Christ. I mulled over this passage and thought, *This is the key—persistent praise and giving thanks in the midst of all things.*

The next time a difficulty arose, I determined that I would praise God in the midst of it—praising Him *in* all things, not *for* all things, because some of the things coming against me were not the will of God but spiritual warfare. I was shocked at the results! Praising God in the middle of a trial really brings exciting answers to prayer.

For instance, one day I was cooking food for the family when I remembered that some guests of our church were in town for a visit. I thought it would be nice to invite them home to eat with us after the service. Looking down at the meager amount of food before me, I decided that I was going to put into practice what I had learned from my Bible study on praising God in the midst of all things. Right then I started singing my own song of praise: "Father, I thank you that you are the God of provision. Thank you right now for the multiplication of this food. I bless you and thank you, God!"

When our guests arrived, I didn't announce that we were

going to be eating small portions. I just knew from my time of praise that God would prepare a banquet table for both our friends and us. I started serving up plates and praising God over each portion and, in the end, we had plenty of food for all. Then, after we ate, I shared what I had done. It was fun and exciting, and we all rejoiced together at the goodness of God.

I have employed the spiritual principle of thanking and praising God in the middle of very difficult situations over the years of my life. I often add Romans 8:28 to my praise during trying times by saying out loud a prayer such as this:

> Father God, I thank you and praise you that this is going to turn for my good. It is impossible for it to be otherwise. I trust and rejoice that you are, at this moment, releasing your provision and blessing into this situation. I choose to rejoice in you, God, and let your praises continually be in my mouth.

This kind of intercessory praise releases God's power into and through the situation where I am challenged. Through these times, God creates new things for my good that I could never have dreamed or imagined for myself while in the midst of the trial. Try it. It works!

Harp and Bowl Intercession

The bringing together of praise and prayer has swept the face of the earth in the prayer movement; it's often called harp and bowl intercession. This marriage of prayer and praise is exemplified in Revelation 5:8–9:

> And when He had taken the scroll, the four living creatures and the twenty-four elders [of the heavenly Sanhedrin]

prostrated themselves before the Lamb. Each was holding a harp (lute or guitar), and they had golden bowls full of incense (fragrant spices and gums for burning), which are the prayers of God's people (the saints). And [now] they sing a new song.

AMP

Harp and bowl intercessory praise and prayer meetings, on a twenty-four-hour basis, are often called 24/7 houses of prayer. Pastor and prayer leader Mike Bickle has been used of God to form International Houses of Prayer (IHOPs) around the globe. Other people have heard the Lord and begun what I call cause intercessory houses of prayer, such as Lou Engle's JHOPs (Justice Houses of Prayer), which pray for the end of legalized abortion and the eradication of human trafficking and slavery. Intercessor and author Pete Greig relates in his book *Red Moon Rising* how the 24/7 prayer movement is changing nations across the face of the earth.

As Mike and I look back to that Marriage of Prayer and Praise gathering in Washington, D.C., in 1986, we can see that, indeed, something was released around the world during that time. The two became one. They already were one theologically, but now they have become one in practice. We know that we were not the only ones receiving revelation about this type of harp and bowl intercession, but we also believe that the 1986 gathering was part of the ushering in of this move of God.

As mentioned earlier, Dick Eastman, the international president of Every Home for Christ (EHC), is one of the greatest prayer warriors I have ever met. He has written a trilogy of books on intercessory worship entitled the Harp and Bowl series. Before I quote from one of the books, let me tell you a little bit about the Jericho Center, the headquarters building for EHC.

Every Home for Christ is an evangelistic ministry whose

mission is to reach every household on the globe with Christian literature. EHC knows that they cannot evangelize the world without the engine of intercessory worship. If you take an elevator to the second floor of the Jericho Center, you will enter two rooms that are side by side. One has a beautiful harp etched in glass on the door; this is used for intercessory worship. They other room is the bowl room and is for more verbal prayers.

If you take the elevator down, you will find the Watchman Center, which includes a beautiful replica of the Wailing Wall in Jerusalem made from beautiful stone found in the Holy Land. There are rooms set aside to intercede for specific locations and regions, such as the Silk Road and the Back to Jerusalem movement (committed to sending 100,000 missionaries to preach the gospel from Asia to Jerusalem).

It is no wonder that EHC is seeing thousands of people receive Christ every day across the face of the earth. While they are blanketing whole nations, house to house with gospel literature, there is a spiritual nuclear plant back home, breaking open the darkness and seeing that every one of those gospel tracts is anointed by God.

The beautiful prayer center at EHC's headquarters is simply an extension of Dick Eastman's personal prayer life. In the third book of the Harp and Bowl series, *Rivers of Delight* (Regal Books), he tells how God called him to a forty-day fast focused on worship and centered on the verse "Delight yourself also in the Lord, and He shall give you the desires of your heart" (Psalm 37:4).

The desire of Dick's heart is clear; he really believes Psalm 2:8: "Ask of Me, and I will give You the nations for Your inheritance, and the ends of the earth for Your possession."

The Praise of a Thousand Villages

I would have to say that if I have a life verse that I love more than any other, it is Psalm 2:8. Maybe you are like me: The thought of millions of people going to eternal damnation without a Savior brings tears to my eyes and makes my heart burn for souls. It seems to me that the thought of God calling Dick to a forty-day worship-based fast is part of the "new wine" move of God. As we worship God in intercessory praise and ask for souls bound in darkness to come to Christ, I believe nations will be transformed around the world.

In *Heights of Delight,* Dick Eastman tells the story of his love for Africa and a vision that he had while praying for missionaries to be sent to Zimbabwe. He recounts this example of passionate love for the lost:

> It was 1839, and 26-year-old David Livingstone sat at a meeting of the London Missionary Society. Robert Moffat, home after an exhaustive missionary tenure in Africa, was pleading for would-be missionaries to pick up the mantle of missions and come to "the dark continent." Painting a word picture of the vast darkness of unevangelized Africa, Moffat declared: "I have sometimes seen, in the morning sun, the smoke of a thousand villages where no missionary has been."
>
> Almost immediately Livingstone picked up Moffat's mantle and within 24 months had settled in Kuruman (located in today's South Africa), Moffat's own field of witness. It was 1841, and three years later Livingstone was to marry Robert Moffat's daughter, Mary; the rest of the story is remarkable missions history.

Dick goes on to recount the impression he had while praying for missionaries to Zimbabwe:

And so it was, a century and a half later that I was mentally seeing a picture—or so it seemed—similar to the one Moffat saw in 1839. I was looking at the smoke of many thousands of villages, not Moffat's "thousand."

"Lord," I said with concern, "are there yet that many villages where the gospel has not reached?"

"No," was the instant impression on my heart, "you are not seeing the smoke of the villages where the gospel has never been heard. You are seeing the smoke of the incense of worship rising from thousands and thousands of villages now transformed by my glory. You are seeing villages that have become worship centers of my presence."

According to Dick, "Intercessory worship refers to concentrated worship that becomes intercessory in nature because it carries the prayers of God's people, like the fragrance of incense, before God's throne. As a result, God releases His power to accomplish His purposes for the harvest."[4]

Although Africa is being reached for Christ, there are still many mission fields around the world where the sound of concentrated worship is not heard, and we need to "stand in the gap" for such nations as Turkmenistan, Azerbaijan, and nations in the Middle East. I am longing for many "musicianaries" to be raised up around the world who will take the praises of God to the darkest parts of the earth.

Whether on a personal level or at the level of reaching nations, the power of persistent praise breaks open the heavens and brings great change. There is no force on earth that will stop our purpose and destiny—either personally or corporately—when we rejoice and give thanks in all things.

Chapter Eight

Intergenerational Prayer

*H*ave you ever read the Bible through in one year? If so, you've come across those long lists of names that can make you want to take a nap from boredom. Perhaps you've thought, *Why would God inspire the writers of Scripture to put all these lineages into these books?* You know, the ones like, "Now this is the genealogy of the sons of Noah: Shem, Ham, and Japheth. And sons were born to them after the flood" (Genesis 10:1).

You might be asking yourself at this point, "OK, Cindy, where are you going with these questions?" One day, while I was reading these lists of names in my Bible, I suddenly had a flash of inspiration: "Oh, I understand: It's about lineage! Family lines are important to God. He loves family!"

The Bible is a book about families. As I turned the pages, I read the subtitles—*The family of Adam, The family of Noah,* etc. In fact, God created us because He wanted a family.

As I was praying about what to include in this book, I felt strongly that I was to write about God's love for lineage and family, and more specifically, the importance of generations praying together. By that I literally mean children, parents, grandparents, and great-grandparents in prayer together. But I am also talking about those of us who are bound together spiritually, by being born again into the family of God. In both cases, we need to have talks with our Father on an intergenerational basis.

Generations are important to God. Remember that He calls himself the God of Abraham, Isaac, and Jacob (Exodus 3:6; Matthew 22:32). What was God's promise to Abraham?

> And in you all the families of the earth shall be blessed.
>
> Genesis 12:3

When many people think of what we call family, they only consider those with whom they are genetically connected. But there is a tie that God gives that blesses both our physical families and our spiritual ones as well.

In the biblical understanding of the word *family*, or *meesh-pah-chah* (Strong's #4940), there is an understanding that it consists not only of a clan or immediate family, but it can extend to as broad a unit as a whole nation.[1]

Mike and I have had the privilege of participating in many prayer meetings around the world. One thing we have noted is that most prayer meetings are made up of intercessors over the age of forty. Others are mostly made up of young people. Children are rarely seen or heard of in intercessory prayer gatherings.

This is what I think needs to happen: The generations need to pray together! We need to pray intergenerationally in a way that includes three generations. God longs to express himself as the God of Abraham, Isaac, and Jacob through our prayers. While I have heard many people talk about this need, I have seen few people who have actually worked to see it function on a regular basis.

Since God expresses himself intentionally as a generational God, doesn't it make sense that special focus needs to be given to see families praying together—whether they are physically or spiritually related? This means we need to light the family altars at home and in the church. The family needs to pray all together.

Let the Children Pray!

One of the most powerful manifestations of intergenerational prayer I have ever seen occurred during an intercessory gathering in Washington, D.C., in the late 1990s. Many prayer groups and leaders were gathered in the nation's capital to pray for nationwide revival. During these meetings, the Holy Spirit was moving in the area of repentance as we came before His throne. The children had been having their own prayer service in the morning, and then we held a combined time of prayer in the afternoon.

The prayer leader for the children was a woman named Esther Ilnisky, author of *Let the Children Pray* (Regal Books). Esther was and is passionate about getting children involved in prayer, both personally and corporately. She is quick to let people know that there is no "junior" Holy Spirit, and that He can pray through a child as well as an adult.

Esther had trained the children to be bold in their prayers. They were not timid or shy; in short, they prayed as well as we could and were bold in their prayer leadership.

I'll never forget their prayers that day in that church in Washington, D.C. One really cute six-year-old African-American girl stood up to pray. Her prayer actually startled me because of the topic she chose. "God," she began, her voice ringing out across the sanctuary, "let them teach in our schools that the boys need to be with girls and the girls with boys." Her prayer was earnest and heartfelt.

As she prayed, my mind spun back to when I was six years old. There was no need to pray such a prayer for my school. No teacher would have dreamed of teaching anything contrary to social norms. Of course, homosexuality was not an issue when I was a child. My next emotion was one of deep repentance because of the huge moral chasm between biblical truth and our educational system today. It is so deep and wide that even a six-year-old child was disturbed by the abandonment of biblical worldview. Frankly, my generation needed to hear that prayer as a wake-up call.

As many of you know, the South American nation of Argentina has experienced a strong revival over the past several decades. The nation seems to have a new move of revival each decade. One of the hallmarks of the Argentine revival has been the number of children directly involved in prayer for the nation. I'll never forget the day I was ministering at a meeting in Buenos Aries. The children involved had spent five hours in the main plaza that day crying out to God for salvations and miracles.

Those children, like the six-year-old in Washington, D.C., also knew how to pray God-sized, faith-filled prayers. In fact, I heard that during their five-hour outdoor prayer meeting, the power of God fell so strongly that people started falling over under the convicting power of God.

When I arrived at the meeting that night, I was told that many of the adults had been "struck to the ground" and couldn't get up until they prayed with the children to receive Christ. As I listened in amazement, I thought to myself, *Esther Ilnisky is right—there is no junior-sized Holy Spirit!*

The miracles that night were extraordinary. I would say they were more on the order of wonders. Argentine evangelist Carlos Annacondia says that miracles are called "signs and wonders" because some of them simply *are* a wonder: They can be explained in no other terms.

I love what Psalm 8:1-2 says:

> God, brilliant Lord, yours is a household name.
> Nursing infants gurgle choruses about you;
> toddlers shout the songs
> that drown out enemy talk,
> and silence atheist babble.

THE MESSAGE

That night the prayers and praises of God's children certainly drowned out what the enemy had done in people's lives. But let's not overlook the intergenerational beauty of what happened that day in Argentina. Someone had to teach those children to pray. Then the adults needed to believe in the power of the children's prayers and take them outside to a plaza for a time of intercession. And that intercession not only prepared the way for the night's meeting but also helped change the spiritual atmosphere and prepare the way for God to bring many people to salvation.

Intergenerational Prayer Mentors

We need prayer mentors who will be intergenerational prayer coaches. I mentioned Dick Eastman's Harp and Bowl series earlier in the book. In one of the three books, *Pathways of Delight,* he writes about the value of mentors and illustrates the value of mentorship from the biblical example of the musicians David appointed for the tabernacle:

> First, the worshipers were mentored. There is something significant in the expression, "All these men were under the direction of their fathers as they made music at the house of the Lord."
>
> 1 Chronicles 25:6 nlt

Eastman goes on to say,

> Something of the origin of the word "mentor" might help us understand its intended meaning. Mentor was actually a character in Homer's poetic classic *The Odyssey.* Mentor was the loyal friend and advisor to the king of Ithaca. Mentor did not spend just a few hours a week with the king's son—he lived with him in Ithaca while the king was gone.

Second, Eastman further expounds by saying that the worshipers were supported. This insight stands out in the text:

> All these men were under the direction of their fathers as they made music at the house of the Lord. . . . They and their families were all trained in making music before the Lord.
>
> 1 Chronicles 25:6–7 nlt

His last excellent point on mentoring from this same chapter is about the diversity of generations represented: "The musicians were appointed . . . without regard to whether they were young or old, teacher or student" (v. 8).[2]

There were families represented in the tabernacle of David, as well as mentors who helped build strength, integrity, and skill.

Many intercessors in my generation need to look for those young people and children whom they can spiritually parent in the house of prayer. This kind of mentoring must be intentional. A generational divide still exists in the church and must be broken down if we are to see the full power of intergenerational agreement. We are yet to see the full potential of the power of God upon families, churches, and nations that comes from this kind of prayer.

I believe that intercession is not so much taught as caught. We need mentors who will pray with other generations on a regular basis in order to impart the blessing and richness that is the result of the Abrahams, Isaacs, and Jacobs praying together.

The first week of 1990, a group of prayer leaders met in Bradenton, Florida, to intercede for the decade. We called it "ninety hours to pray for the '90s." We prayed for a great harvest of souls—especially among the Jews and Arabs.

One of my special delights was interceding with the great prayer warrior Joy Dawson. She is a specialist on praying the Word. I will never forget sitting in a circle with other leaders from different generations late into the night. The first thing she would ask us to do was to study a certain passage of Scripture concerning a particular nation. The next thing would be to ask the Holy Spirit to show us how to pray from the passage concerning that region of the world.

Then we would share with one another what we were hearing from the Lord. There were times when Joy would ask us to stop and examine our hearts toward the people for whom we were about to intercede. Were we prepared to pray from a pure heart? Was there any unforgiveness in our hearts? On a corporate level, did we have any prejudice concerning the people for whom we were to stand in the gap?

After this time of preparation, we were at last ready to pray. Often Joy would again ask us to stop and quietly and carefully listen to the Lord to hear what He would have us express in intercession before the throne of God.

I believe great leaders were birthed out of those ninety hours of prayer and intergenerational connection. Many people were impacted and received impartation from great generals of intercession like Joy Dawson. I'll never forget those lessons in the school of prayer.

To review, here are some of the points we learned in our ninety hours of prayer, which are transferable to many prayer contexts (not only intergenerational prayer):

1. Study the Scripture passages relating to the subject you want to focus on in your prayer time.
2. Spend time in quiet introspection before the Lord to prepare to pray.
3. Share with others in your group what God is showing you through your time of preparation.
4. Bring your requests before the throne of God.
5. Pray with faith, expecting God to answer.

It is a biblical truth that the generations should teach one another. In my opinion, shouldn't we see this done through our intercession as well?

I am passionate about intergenerational impartation, and the following passage accurately depicts this wonderful aspect of being a follower of Jesus:

> We will tell the next generation the praiseworthy deeds of
> the Lord, his power, and the wonders he has done. He decreed
> statutes for Jacob and established the law in Israel, which he

commanded our forefathers to teach their children, so the
next generation would know them, even the children yet to
be born, and they in turn would tell their children. Then they
would put their trust in God and would not forget his deeds,
but would keep his commands.

PSALM 78:4–7 NIV

Of course, not only is there a great blessing when our spiritual
parents bless us, but how wonderful it is when our own biological
grandparents bless us as well. Toward this point, indulge me, if
you will, with yet another family story:

A number of years ago, I was speaking for a women's chapter
of Aglow International in my birthplace of San Antonio, Texas.
Since my mother still lived there along with her husband, Tom,
and my grandmother, I stayed in their home.

By this time my grandmother must have been at least in
her early nineties. I was late getting home one night because we
went out to eat after the meeting. As I tiptoed into the house,
conscious of not wanting to wake my family, I noticed a figure
kneeling down by her bed. It was Grandmother McJilton.

"Grandma," I queried, "What are you doing?" I probably
wouldn't have asked her, but because of her age, I wanted to
make sure she was all right.

"Oh, Cindy, you're home!" she exclaimed with joy. "I was
concerned for you and was praying for your safety."

I went quickly to hug and kiss her, smelling the sweet gardenia
powder she always wore. Even though she has been in heaven
for many years, I can still feel the loving comfort of her prayers
that day deep in my heart and soul.

My dear friend Quin Sherrer has written many wonderful
books. One of the sweetest is written from her own life story,
Prayers from a Grandma's Heart.

Quin says that *to bless* in the biblical sense also means "to ask for or to impart supernatural favor." When we ask God to bless our grandchildren, we are crying out for the wonderful unlimited goodness that only God has the power to give them. How loved children must feel to have grandparents pray over them, bless them, and impart love in a special way.[3]

My godly grandmother went on to be with the Lord when she was almost one hundred years old. The last time I saw her she was in a care home. I had slipped in to say good-bye but was stopped by the sound of her voice at the door of her room. Arrested in my tracks by the authority in her voice, I gazed in wonder at her lying prone with her eyes shut. She had no idea I was even there.

"What is right and what is wrong," she spoke with a loud cry. "To love God with your whole heart, soul, and mind. That is what is right."

That was the last time I saw her, but she left behind a priceless gift for her family generations—to love God with everything within us. Thank you, Grandmother, for this legacy.

In 2 Timothy, Paul encourages Timothy and points to the faith of his mother and grandmother:

> I have been reminded of your sincere faith, which first lived in your grandmother Lois and in your mother Eunice and, I am persuaded, now lives in you also.
>
> 2 TIMOTHY 1:5 NIV

Leaving a Generational Blessing

Generational praying, or intercession for the generations to come, leaves a treasure of God that deposits an intergenerational blessing. The following story is a great example:

When George McLuskey married and started a family, he

decided to pray for one hour a day for his kids to follow Christ. After a time, he expanded his prayers to include his grandchildren and great-grandchildren. Every day between eleven and noon, he prayed for the three generations.

As the years went by, his two daughters committed their lives to Christ and married men who went into full-time ministry. The two couples produced four girls and one boy. Each of the girls married a minister, and the boy became a pastor. The first two grandchildren born to this generation were both boys. Upon graduation from high school, the two cousins chose the same college and became roommates. During their sophomore year, one boy decided to go into the ministry. The other didn't. He undoubtedly felt some pressure to continue in the family legacy, but chose instead to pursue his interest in psychology. He earned a doctorate and eventually wrote books for parents, titles that became bestsellers. He started a radio program heard on more than a thousand stations each day. The man's name—James Dobson.[4] James went on to found the organization called Focus on the Family, the largest family-based Christian organization in the world.

As young parents, Mike and I always prayed each night with our children. We had our routine: For some reason, we usually chose Daniel's bed for our nightly prayers. Each child, starting with Daniel, the youngest, would pray out loud. Mike would finish last. Those are still some of my sweetest memories.

Each morning and all throughout the day, I pray for my children and grandchildren, and I am sure there will be a great legacy that God will pass down from Mike and me through our generations.

Even if you do not have a godly heritage like James Dobson, you can begin now, in your lifetime. If you aren't married, you can pray for your nieces or nephews, or "adopt" children in intercession. I have a friend who is a missionary and, although she has never had biological children, she is still a "grandmother" to the children of the young people she has led to the Lord. She prays for her spiritual legacy on a regular basis. This is important because God sets the solitary in families (Psalm 68:6).

If you are single, I encourage you to do a similar thing. Find some young people from your church or community and "adopt" them in prayer. It will really bless them if you tell them what you are doing, if they are in a place to want to hear it. Who knows, you may end up with a whole "adopted" family through your intercession for them!

Another idea is for local churches to intentionally pair up the generations to pray for one another. This can be done through the women's organizations working with the youth and children's ministries. The men's ministry could also take the same approach. Many great ideas never happen because there isn't a person who is willing to take on the assignment. Don't wait for someone else; determine that you will be the answer. Sometimes the need is the call.

My good friend Cheryl Sacks writes about a mentoring prayer relationship that God gave her as a young woman. She says:

> I had just moved back to Texas from Florida to be with my mom after the tragic death of my father. I was devastated, without a job, and seeking the Lord for my next step. I was fortunate to have a praying mother, and one added benefit was that her best friend, Hazel, wanted to spend time with me—to help me develop my faith and prayer life. She never told me that was her intention and she never used the word mentor. I certainly had no idea I was being mentored. But I suspect Hazel knew exactly what she was doing. For about seven months, Hazel and I spent part of almost every day together. Sometimes we went out to lunch, for coffee, or for a walk in

the mall. Much of the time we attended Bible studies and Christian services. Each time we were together, Hazel asked, "How are you doing? How can I pray for you? Is there anything I can do for you?"[5]

Cheryl has gone on to be a minister, author, and major voice in the prayer movement of America. I wonder what would have happened to Cheryl without Hazel's influence in her life. Cheryl also has a godly mother who intercedes for her on a regular basis. When you take the step to give encouragement and pray for the next generation, you never know how God might use that person, or what will become of your investment.

God's house should be a place of prayer for all generations. Sadly, our prayer meetings are usually the most generationally segregated times of the week. Even if the children come, they are often taken to the nursery, or if they stay we observe the adage that children should be seen and not heard. I agree with Esther Ilnisky: *Let the children pray!* Not only that, the children should see the youth pray, and the youth should pray with the adults. Then we will have truly become a "house of prayer for all nations."

Of course, each generation needs time to pray by itself. This is necessary as well. One cannot expect a child or youth to pray out loud who has never been mentored in peer-level intercession. Churches need to think about putting as much emphasis on establishing "pray grounds" as they do playgrounds. There are many fun and exciting children's prayer tools. One is a soft globe that children toss from child to child. When they catch the ball they cry out, "I pray for all the children in Iraq!" or whatever country their hands land upon. Songs about prayer are powerful in intercession as well. Maps of the world could be painted on the floor of their "pray grounds," and the children could then stand on a particular nation and intercede for it.

For corporate prayer, think beforehand how you can integrate all the generations into your time of intercession. Perhaps you might want to contact the parents of various children, or talk to the children's pastor to see which ones have been used by God in their own prayer meetings to voice their prayers publicly. Intergenerational praying is fun and rewarding. Let's make our house—whether our home or our church house—a biblical House of Prayer for all Nations. There will be great fruit to our children and our children's children.

Isn't it exciting to think of the book of remembrance that God might be writing for your family and church? The generations will rise up and call you blessed for what you might do for them by establishing a prayer legacy. I can see mine now—*and Grandmother prayed for Malachi, Caden, Zion, and Lilli, (including any future grandchildren or great-grandchildren), and each of them became great in the kingdom of God.* For Mike and me, this is our dream. Why don't you establish an intergenerational prayer legacy of your own?

Chapter Nine

Proclamation Prayer

proc·la·ma·tion—something *proclaimed; specifically*: an official formal public announcement

*P*roclamation prayer is decreeing the will of God done on earth as it is in heaven. It brings God's will to earth, as it is in heaven. The Lord's Prayer is a type of this praying (Matthew 6:9–13). It can yield dramatic results!

Bill Johnson, author and pastor of Bethel Church in Redding, California, took a team from his church into the city of Tijuana, Mexico. Their time in Tijuana is an excellent demonstration of how proclamation prayer can bring God's intervention to a city.

The team met at six in the evening on a stage near central Tijuana, on a street that houses prostitutes, gangs, and a rampant drug trade. As the team entered into a wonderful and powerful time of prayer and worship, people from the surrounding area began to gather around. It wasn't unlike when in the book of

Acts, people gathered around the people of God to see what was happening in the Spirit.

Rain, however, had been threatening most of the day and started to fall shortly after the prayer ministry began. Bobby Brown, one of the young leaders of the church, knew that if the rain continued, it would take away from what he felt God wanted to accomplish that night. Grabbing the microphone, he told the crowd that God was going to stop the rain. As he spoke, he then prayed a quick prayer and the rain stopped, leaving the crowd both amazed and wondering how it could have happened. People couldn't help but be drawn in. One look at the crowd revealed their desire for God's presence and a deep longing for a revelation of His love.

For six hours the team preached, received words of knowledge, led people to the Lord, and saw many miracles of healing. It was as if what was happening had a momentum of its own, because it was beyond comprehension. The team was co-laboring with God, the kingdom was coming, and the team was simply a vessel for seeing the gospel do its work. There were at least six altar calls, but even between asking people if they wanted to receive Jesus, the team connected with people surrounding the stage. More than one hundred people received Christ that night, including five prostitutes, an immigrant from Iran, and a man whose eye had been gouged out in a fight.[1]

The kind of proclamation praying demonstrated by Bobby Brown may seem unusual to some people in the church today. However, it is entirely biblical to pray in this manner. Bobby was co-laboring with God through intercession to see His will done in that particular area, and stopping the rain was part of the kingdom advancement that night.

What if Bobby had not taken authority over the rain that evening through proclamation praying? Most likely more than one hundred people would still be bound for a dark eternity. At the very least, their release from captivity would have been delayed. This makes me wonder how many times we could have seen the power of God manifested in supernatural ways through prayer, but we didn't know how to intercede in a manner that would stop the plan of Satan and advance the purpose of God.

The Tijuana story highlights what can happen when just one person steps out in faith. For this determined young man, a downpour was not going to stop the will of God from being done at a time when he and his team believed God had called them to harvest souls for the kingdom of God.

Proclaiming God's Will on Earth

The good news is that you can learn to proclaim God's will on the earth as well. Proclamation prayers are a form of intercession where God's will is decreed over a given situation and anything contrary is brought into alignment. Do you want to know how to pray like that? The first step in proclamation praying is to realize that you have an active role in seeing God's will done on the earth. The praying church is God's governmental body on earth.

About fifteen years ago, I came across the Scripture that I quoted earlier, Matthew 6:10, during my regular Bible reading. I had prayed the Lord's Prayer many times before, but never believed that God wanted His kingdom to come in any manner during my lifetime. I always equated the kingdom of God with heaven.

Many of us around the world know that there is a future kingdom but there is also a present kingdom. In order to see His kingdom come, we have to do our part to make it so! This is especially true when it comes to intercession and proclamation praying, which is one of the most powerful tools we have to see this happen.

When we proclaim and decree God's will through intercession, we are functioning in our created role as the church, or *ekklesia*. The role we have as the praying church on the earth is actually governmental in nature. By this I mean that God has called us and given us authority as believers to govern (i.e., oversee, rule, and manage) the earth according to His will. Notice the first mention of the church by Jesus:

> I also say to you that you are Peter, and on this rock I will build My church, and the gates of Hades shall not prevail against it. And I will give you the keys of the kingdom of heaven, and whatever you bind on earth will be bound in heaven, and whatever you loose on earth will be loosed in heaven.
>
> MATTHEW 16:18–19

Dutch Sheets says this about the passage in his excellent book *Authority in Prayer:*

> When Jesus used the word church (Greek: ekklesia), the disciples weren't hindered by our contemporary preconceived ideas as to what it meant. Their paradigm of an ekklesia differed greatly from what it has become. To us today it is (1) a worship service; (2) a building used by Christians; (3) a local congregation of Christians; or (4) for those who tend toward a more literal meaning, the people of God, "called out" from the world. The last concept is the most accurate, according to a strict translation, but it still falls short of communicating what an ekklesia was when Christ made His stunning announcement.
>
> To the Greeks in Christ's day an *ekklesia* was an assembly of people set apart to govern the affairs of a state or nation— in essence, a parliament or congress. To the Romans it was a group of people sent into a conquered region to *alter the culture* [italics mine], until it became like Rome. Realizing this was

the ideal way to control the empire, they infiltrated government, social structures, language, schools, etc., until the people talked, thought, and acted like Romans.[2]

Today, we are Christ's ekklesia—we are His governing body on the earth to see His will accomplished. If we don't govern through intercession, the gates of Hades prevail. In biblical times, Hades was a place greatly feared in Asia Minor. I did quite a bit of research on this topic for my book *Deliver Us from Evil.* The authority that we, the ekklesia, have over evil's power is stated in Ephesians 4:8–10: "Therefore He says: 'When He ascended on high, He led captivity captive, and He gave gifts to men.' "

"He ascended." What does it mean but that Jesus also first *descended* into the lower parts of the earth? He who descended is also the One who ascended far above all the heavens that He might fill all things.

The book of Ephesians is full of statements of authority. When one studies the words in the Greek, coupled with the knowledge of the number of gods the Greeks worshiped, it gives you an idea of how powerful a statement is being made in this passage. God is literally saying to us, "I have given you gifts to overcome the worst and most feared powers of darkness through my name so you can fill all things."

The Keys to Binding and Loosing

Christ led "captivity captive" by first descending into the lower parts of the earth. His subsequent departure clearly shows that Christ overthrew the dominion of Hades, the underworld, or what the Old Testament calls *Sheol.*[3]

In Paul's day, these spirits of Hades had names such as *Hekate*. This particular goddess of the underworld was revered and considered to have authority over "the keys to Hades."[4] Christ descended into Hades and took these keys away from Satan and all the powers of the underworld and gave them to us to wield as His governing body on the earth (Matthew 16:19; Revelation 1:18).

With these keys we can bind and loose those things that Satan is trying to use to establish his governing rule on the earth. We can even teach little children that they do not need to be afraid, because they have been given this kind of authority over the world of darkness.

I wish I had been aware of this fact as a little girl. As a child, I was very afraid of vampires. I would hide under the covers at night and make a small breathing hole, thinking that they would not be able to see me. I don't know how I thought they would miss that kid-sized lump on the bed! But even in my child-sized body, I could have thrown those covers off and proclaimed, "In the name of Jesus, I don't have to be afraid of you, spirit of fear! It is written that I can resist the devil and he will flee from me!"

God's authority is always available, even to frightened little girls (James 4:7). Isn't it great that we can teach our children not to be afraid because we have been given the keys of the kingdom and authority over fear?

We need to understand that we can pray proclamation prayers with authority and that our prayers can help bring things on earth into kingdom order. This should begin with us from the time we are little children trying to fall asleep in the dark, until we become adults and wield great authority over spiritual darkness that is encroaching into our cities and nations.

Secondly, as members of God's *ekklesia*, or governing body on the earth, and through our use of the keys of the kingdom of heaven, we have the power to discern those things that are trying to stop God's will from being done.

Keys are used for locking and unlocking doors. One must find the right key to unlock a specific door—not just any key will work. The kingdom keys that open locked doors were given to us by Jesus Christ himself when He ascended into heaven—the keys to unlock His will on earth so the will of God fills all things. We cannot use natural wisdom: It is God's Word, and the knowledge of His will in any given situation, that helps us know what to open and what to shut.

Proclamation prayers open closed doors. Our voice, under the power of the Holy Spirit, decrees His will. By proclamation we decree and either bind or loose.

Pastor and author Gary Kinnaman offers this theological basis for binding and loosing: The use of *binding* and *loosing* did not, in fact, originate with Jesus. It was a frequent expression of first-century Jewish rabbinical dialect. According to Alexander Bruce in *The Expositor's Greek New Testament*, to *bind* and *loose*—Greek: *deo* and *luo*—meant simply "to prohibit" and "to permit," that is, to establish (Vol. 1, 225). The Jewish authorities at the time of Christ retained the right to establish guidelines for, or keys to, religious practice and social interaction. But *deo* (bind) also expresses *"supernatural control."* In Luke 13:15–16, Jesus rebuked a Jewish leader: "You hypocrites! Doesn't each of you on the Sabbath untie (*luo* [loose]) his ox or donkey from the stall and lead it out to give it water? Then should not this woman, a daughter of Abraham, whom Satan has kept bound for eighteen long years, be set free (*luo* [loose]) on the Sabbath day from what bound her?"[5]

By understanding our authority through His name and Word to proclaim God's will on the earth, it is possible to stay the power of the enemy. When we pray with authority, *all things* become subject to God's kingdom rule.

Taking Hold of Our Authority in Christ

Our training for kingdom intercession through proclamation praying must begin on a personal level, and then we will learn to function as an *ekklesia* in intercession. Evidently Bill and Beni Johnson have taught their students well their authority in Christ, as evidenced in the opening story of this chapter. We will go more deeply into functioning in our *ekklesia* role in the last chapter, "Kingdom Intercession."

It may seem strange to some that the young leader from Bill Johnson's church would command the rain to stop. That's not a prayer you hear in church on a typical Sunday! However, it is not at all an anti-biblical prayer. Recall the story of Jesus questioning His disciples' fear and "little faith" in the middle of a storm:

> Now when He got into a boat, His disciples followed Him. And suddenly a great tempest arose on the sea, so that the boat was covered with the waves. But He was asleep. Then His disciples came to Him and awoke Him, saying, "Lord, save us! We are perishing!" But He said to them, "Why are you fearful, O you of little faith?" Then He arose and rebuked the winds and the sea, and there was a great calm.
>
> Matthew 8:23–26

In other words, Jesus is telling His disciples that if their faith had been stronger, they could have taken authority over the storm without His involvement. According to the "Word Wealth" section of the *Spirit-Filled Life Bible*, the words *little faith* are from *oligos*, "small," and *pistos*, "faith" (Strong's #3640), describing a faith that lacks confidence or trusts too little. Another way to term it is "underdeveloped faith," as opposed to outright unbelief or distrust (*apistis*).[6]

Some of us are standing in the midst of life's storms, crying out to God: "Why don't you do something about my situation?" As believers, however, we already have the key to change it! We can bind and loose and take authority over the situation we are currently dealing with in our lives. I am convinced there are times when Jesus looks down on us and says from heaven, "Use the key! Exercise your faith! Speak to the storm to *be still.*"

The incident of the disciples and the storm was not the only time Jesus demonstrated power and authority over creation and exhorted the disciples to have faith. He also did so after He spoke to the fig tree and proclaimed or commanded, saying, "Let no fruit grow on you ever again" (Matthew 21:19).

The disciples were shocked when the fig tree withered away immediately. In fact, the Bible says that they marveled. I would have too! I love the passage of Scripture that follows this occurrence:

> Assuredly, I say to you, if you have faith and do not doubt, you will not only do what was done to the fig tree, but also if you say to this mountain, "Be removed and be cast into the sea," it will be done. And whatever things you ask in prayer, believing, you will receive.
>
> MATTHEW 21:21–22

Note one very important teaching point from this passage: Jesus had made a *proclamation* and equated it with prayer in this case. There are other forms of prayer, but in this instance, Jesus used proclamation prayer. In fact, He teaches that "if you *say* to this mountain, 'Be removed,' it will be done." In this case, the *saying* in faith was a form of *praying*.

As a young mother in my thirties, I had heard some teaching on taking authority over creation through the name of Jesus. I had been meditating during my devotions on the passage from Matthew 21 on asking in faith.

It was a hot summer day in El Paso, Texas, and I started running the hose to water my plants so they would survive the brutal desert heat. After a while I ran outside, remembering that I needed to turn off the water. To my dismay, the faucet handle was swarming with thirsty bees, taking advantage of the spray coming from the poor connection of faucet to hose. I thought, "Well, I have authority over those bees!" and started rebuking them.

After a moment I stopped, chagrined that they were not paying the least bit of attention to my proclamation to depart! I went back inside and turned on the Christian radio station while I cleaned my house. One teacher after another was expounding on the message of faith.

All of a sudden, I leapt up, full of faith, and ran outside, proclaiming, "In the name of Jesus: Bees, leave the faucet!" All at once the bees took flight and I was able to turn off the faucet. It was great that I could shut off the water, but what else happened? My little faith became large faith and produced great results.

Dutch Sheets gives us a list of things over which Jesus demonstrated ownership and authority while on the earth:

1. He established authority over the laws of nature, walking on water (Matthew 14:25).

2. He controlled the forces of nature, altering weather patterns (Mark 4:39).

3. He trumped the laws of physics, multiplying food, turning water into wine, translating His physical body from one place to another, and destroying trees simply by speaking to them (Matthew 15:36; John 2:9; 6:20–21; Mark 11:13–14, 20).

4. He demonstrated authority over the animal world, using a fish to collect money needed for a tax (Matthew 17:27).

5. He had dominion over disease, healing multitudes (Acts 10:38).

6. He even displayed power over death, bringing the dead back to life (John 11:43–44).[7]

Stepping Out in Proclamation Prayer

It is important to note that Jesus did not arbitrarily demonstrate authority over these things; there was divine reasoning behind His actions. The same principle applies to us today. We might have authority given to us over nature, but we do not have the right at any given moment to disrupt the earth's weather patterns for our own selfish reasons. In the case of the bees and the water faucet, I needed to turn off the water or my plants would have been ruined and my water bill would have been sky high.

It is also important that we do not pray proclamation prayers presumptively. For instance, you might stand on the banks of a flooding river and make a decree that you are going to walk on water, only to find that you are swimming for your life!

It is good to begin exercising your faith on small things so you will be able to make bolder proclamation prayers when needed, such as the outreach conducted by Bill Johnson's team in Tijuana.

Through the years, I have grown in my faith levels in prayer, and in my understanding and use of proclamation praying. One dramatic example of proclamation prayer took place during a large prayer gathering called the Call Nashville, which occurred on July 7, 2007.

More than 70,000 youth and prayer leaders gathered in a large outdoor sports stadium in Nashville, Tennessee, to pray for the United States. The Call is headed up by a man named Lou Engle, who passionately fights for the rights of unborn children. While there were many causes we prayed about that day, the fight to end abortion was certainly a central theme.

The day was hot. The kind of heat that makes you want to be certain you never go to "that place of eternal judgment"! While the prayer was strong and fervent, one could tell that the crowd was feeling the tremendous heat. The team kept passing out bottles of water and encouraging everyone to stay hydrated, but people were dropping like flies under the scorching sun.

Finally Lou came to me backstage and said, "Cindy, the authorities want to shut us down because so many people are passing out. Please do something." I knew that he meant pray, but how do you pray for such a thing? I paced up and down on the platform for a few minutes and then I knew what to do. I looked around for a young person with whom I could partner to do some serious proclamation praying, someone to pull into the gap with me. The young man I approached was very radical-looking. I could tell he was exactly the right person by the manner in which he'd been praying throughout the morning.

"Come with me!" I instructed (rather imperially, in retrospect). He didn't hesitate for a second, but followed while I quickly shared the situation with him.

Peering up into the sky, we noted that there was not a single cloud in sight—not even a little one from which God could make a larger one.

Looking back, I now know that the training that began with the bees at the water faucet was going to stand me in good stead. I didn't have a doubt in my mind that we were going to have a miracle that day.

How did we pray? I just looked at my prayer partner and said, "Let's kneel down and pray!"

He dropped to his knees like a good soldier of the Lord. And we prayed. After a while I stood up and looked at the sky—nothing. We prayed again, on our knees. Finally I looked at him and said, "Now we are going to point to the sky and command the clouds to come."

This was our proclamation: "In the name of Jesus, we command the clouds to come from the four corners of the earth and cover this stadium. We speak to the north, the south, the east, and the west. *Clouds come!*"

Did they come? Of course they did. After about fifteen minutes we looked up and there were a few clouds, and then more wonderful white, fluffy clouds began to amass across the stadium. At last it was covered in a layer that protected the pray-ers against the extreme heat.

How did God do it? I have no idea.

But that's not all. When that marvelous cloud-cover had been accomplished, I told my young prayer warrior, "Now let's command the winds to blow."

We were both feeling a little giddy and full of faith by that time. Here is our second proclamation prayer: "Father God, we speak to the winds to come! Come from the north, the south, the east, and the west, and blow across this stadium!"

Then came the faith part: I wet my index finger and stuck it in the air in anticipation. And sure enough, within a few minutes I could feel the breeze against the moisture of my finger. The meeting went on without interruption and God's will was accomplished.

Does this all sound crazy to you? Do you think the appearance of clouds and wind that day in Nashville were just coincidence? I can understand your skepticism, but remember, the Bible gives us multiple evidences of Jesus and the Old Testament leaders (e.g., Moses at the Red Sea) using proclamation prayers with regard to the physical elements.

A Look at Declaration Prayer

Our use of proclamation prayer might also include *decreeing* God's will on the earth. A prayer decree is the command that brings God's will into a given situation, declaring something to be either bound (unlawful) or loosed (lawful). A biblical instance of this is found in the powerful passage concerning nations in Psalm 2:7, 10–11:

> I will declare the decree: The Lord has said to Me, "Now therefore, be wise, O kings; be instructed, you judges of the earth. Serve the Lord with fear, and rejoice with trembling."

Note that in this passage a person is being used by God to *decree* into the earth His will. This powerful passage, written by a king, is decreeing the will of God by a prophetic declaration: that the judges of the earth should serve the Lord.

Another psalm of declaration often used in proclamation praying is Psalm 24:7–10:

> Lift up your heads, O you gates! And be lifted up, you everlasting doors! And the King of glory shall come in. Who is this King of glory? The Lord strong and mighty, the Lord mighty in battle. Lift up your heads, O you gates! . . . And the

King of glory shall come in. Who is this King of glory? The
Lord of hosts, He is the King of glory.

On a number of occasions I have stood with prayer partners at
the borders of closed nations and declared this psalm. And there
have been times when the doors seemed like they were sealed shut
in communist countries or other restricted-access nations, and
we used Psalm 24 to help break down the barriers to entry.

Many years ago we felt led by God to travel into a communist
country for a time of strategic prayer and ministry. But within
a day or two before our scheduled departure, our visa approval
had still not come through. Our staff at Generals International
proclaimed from Psalm 24 that the gate to the nation would
open. Shortly thereafter, and with little time to spare, we received
our approvals and were cleared to enter the nation. Would the
visa have come without our proclamation prayer? Perhaps, but
I have known others that have had to either cancel or postpone
missionary trips due to visa complications or delays. I, for one,
believe God moved upon the government leaders whose approval
we needed for the visa.

Tools of Proclamation Prayer

1. Binding and loosing—This prayer will bind the work of
   the enemy and loose the legal will of God into a given
   situation.

2. Scripture proclamation—Choosing appropriate Scripture
   passages to proclaim the will of God.

3. Decrees—Speaking a prophetic word from God in order

to change a current situation that is contrary to the will of God.

4. Declarations—Declaring the will of God under the inspiration and guidance of the Holy Spirit.

Dick Eastman tells this story of when God told him to make a declaration on the campus of his alma mater, North Central Bible College:

Arriving at the chilly Minneapolis campus, I had little idea how to process the strange promise God had give me prior to my arrival: that I would see something new that I had never witnessed before. Prior to the morning chapel rally, the first in the series, God showed me several things I could expect that week. His voice was as clear as usual, and I decided to write the items down, in order that I might share these promises with the student body. The list included ten declarations. Number two stood out above the others: "There will be a wave of sacrifice on this campus unlike anything we have ever witnessed. It will be the beginning of a life of total discipleship."

Standing before the students I read the list. I noticed some students openly whispering and looking at one another, puzzled. I quickly explained that I was as puzzled as they were, and called for cooperation in allowing God to do as He wished. They responded favorably.

The first night of the week came and went. It was certainly one to remember. None left the chapel before midnight.

By the following evening a number of miracles had already happened. The auditorium seemed to be aflame with God's glory. It was the night God promised "a new discipleship" and "a wave of sacrifice."

I was concluding what I felt were my final remarks when a startling thing occurred. A student who had left five minutes earlier returned and was heading straight to the platform. In her hand she gripped a black object. It was her wallet. Standing before a crowded auditorium of classmates, she stepped to the microphone.

"God told me to go and get this from my room. It's all I have. He told me to do it now, before this service ends." She turned to hand me the wallet and stepped awkwardly from the platform.

Suddenly a strong wind of conviction settled upon the four hundred students. Students were coming from everywhere toward the platform. They were emptying their wallets; the majority giving everything they had.

Dollars, however, were not the only things given that night. Students began leaving the chapel moments after conviction settled. Again, only the Holy Spirit prompted them. Within two hours the platform looked like a junkyard—televisions, instruments, albums, radios, sports equipment, photographs, a rifle, and a mink-trimmed coat.[8]

Declaring or decreeing the will of God under the inspiration of the Holy Spirit has the power to change the spiritual climate in a given situation and bring heaven to earth.

Chapter Ten

Kingdom Intercession

On June 1, 2009, Mike and I were in Hong Kong, standing on the helipad of the historic Peninsula Hotel, overlooking the breathtakingly beautiful harbor. Our friend Linda Ma was pointing out the stadium that had been used the day before for the Global Day of Prayer. As I listened to her describe how they had rented the facility, and how they had circled the harbor with thousands of intercessors on twelve different sites, my mind flashed back to the prayer that had gone on the day before. The stadium was packed with Chinese Christians as well as international visitors. A choir of what looked to be at least five hundred voices thundered their praise to Almighty God.

The Global Day of Prayer was started by a businessman from South Africa named Graham Power. This was the ninth year of the global event, and it had grown like wildfire, burning its way across continents. By this last prayer gathering, it had reached a zenith that none could have dreamed years before: People from all 220 nations of the earth gathered to worship and pray in one concerted voice.

One theme emerged and has swept the nations of the earth:

> *O God! Let your kingdom come and your will be done on earth as it is in heaven!*

The prayers that day resounded from believers in the various sectors of society. Leaders in the worldwide prayer movement prefer to call them the seven mountains of society. Various groups wore specific colors to distinguish them in prayer; for example, business people wore one color and educators another. The choir would then hold up large cards reflecting the specific colors, and the thousands of people praying would then pray in agreement for God to touch that respective sector of society.

Again and again prayers such as the following shook heaven and earth: "Father God, we want to see the media dedicated to you and used for the advancement of your kingdom and to glorify your name." Other groups prayed similarly for their respective "mountains" of influence.

The Global Day of Prayer is a perfect example of what I call kingdom intercession, that is, prayer that moves beyond our personal needs to the larger vision for God's kingdom to come around the world. My journey into kingdom intercession began about fifteen years ago, when the Holy Spirit started me on a path of discovery. One day as I was reading my Bible, I came across a Scripture that seemed to leap off of the page:

> And this gospel of the kingdom shall be preached in all the world as a witness to all the nations, and then the end will come.
>
> MATTHEW 24:14

As a follower of Jesus Christ, it has always been my passion to see the power of God touch my neighborhood, my city, and my country. Even as a child, I remember longing for people to come to know Christ. And when I read Matthew 24:14, I was struck with the realization that the reason I had been put on this earth goes far beyond what I had previously understood. It wasn't just about being a follower of Christ on a personal level, but that God wanted to use me—and every believer—to cause the kingdom to advance in all the world.

Activating Kingdom Intercession

Since this is a book about persistent prayer, and thus intercession, Matthew 24 leads us to the question: "How can an ordinary believer like me be part of kingdom intercession to see the gospel advance?" Our desire, then, is to activate Matthew 6:10, a verse that is being prayed in houses of prayer, at assemblies, and in the Global Day of Prayer movement: "Your kingdom come. Your will be done on earth as it is in heaven."

In fact, everything presented in this book so far leads us to this proclamation of the will of God. In order to see the kingdom of God advance in the earth, which is an end-time mandate, we need all the tools we've talked about: praying the Word, fasting, proclaiming, and decreeing. All these weapons in our spiritual arsenal are to be used in kingdom intercession. We've talked in general terms about kingdom intercession, but here is a more precise definition:

> Kingdom intercession is targeted, focused prayer that releases the will of God into every sector of society to see a biblical worldview released into the culture.

For this kind of intercessory prayer to fill the earth, we need an army of prayer warriors to stand in the gap! This includes soccer moms, children in elementary schools and high schools, men and women in business and industry, and workers on the factory floor, each praying for their homes, schools, and businesses each morning. God wants us to fill the earth with prayers to see His will done on earth as it is in heaven, because the job is enormous, and it is going to take a multi-generational red, black, yellow, brown, and white army to do it!

Every year Mike and I have the privilege of speaking to people from nations across the globe, and to hear the exciting stories that they are telling about how they are advancing the kingdom of God. As we have traveled and prayed with nationals from various countries, I have come to understand that we are going to be responsible to God for our nations when we stand before the throne of God. Did we intercede for our nation and its leaders? Did we work on the local, city, state, and national levels to be Christ's hands and feet, seeking justice and righteousness?

A number of years ago my friend Guatemalan pastor Harold Caballeros and I were walking across the grounds of his school in Guatemala City. I asked him, "What is the primary thing that you are teaching the children here?"

Immediately Harold said with joy, "We are instructing them to see Revelation 21:24 fulfilled before the throne for our nation: 'And the nations of those who are saved shall walk in its light, and the kings of the earth bring their glory and honor into it.' Each child is being trained to pray strategically for our country, so that when the great role call of nations is made in heaven, as Guatemalans, we will present it as a saved nation."

A saved nation. That is an interesting concept. How does this tie into kingdom intercession? In order to see a nation saved, one must see a reformation and transformation back to kingdom order and values, or biblical worldview.

Defining a Biblical Worldview

First of all, let's define *worldview*. German social economist Max Weber used terminology related to worldview in his analysis of the relationship between a people's belief system and their level of prosperity or poverty.[1] In other words, what you believe determines your worldview, and your worldview largely determines your lifestyle.

Our worldview as Christians is based upon the Bible. Our job as an *ekklesia*, among other things, is to see the will of God done on earth as it is in heaven. In other words, we endeavor to see heaven's culture invade earth's distinctives until our nation's governmental order is set upon the foundation of the Creator's design.

When I wrote my first book on intercessory prayer in 1991, *Possessing the Gates of the Enemy*, we didn't have a grasp on how to order our intercession into a strategic model according to kingdom of God values (biblical worldview). I wrote how many Christians pray shotgun prayers because they are not focused, and they are not really seeing the results they would like. In contrast, kingdom intercession is targeted and focused.

While we made great advances in the prayer movement through the '80s and '90s, we were still, to some degree, tactical rather than strategic in our intercession. In other words, we prayed here and there and over this and that, rather randomly. What was truly needed was a strategic plan to target specific areas of society in order to see the kingdom of God manifest in the various sectors and spheres of influence.

This is where kingdom intercession is so critical, in that it focuses on various sectors of society to bring massive reformational change.

Since Matthew 6:10 is a rallying cry echoing across the face of the earth, we must develop persistent prayer strategies that can be grasped and presented in a way that will touch children, youth, and adults. There is a future and a present kingdom, and the present one will never come to fruition without our fervent and targeted prayers.

We must learn how we can see our culture and nation filled with the power of the kingdom of God as well as the restoration of biblical truth in other nations. This will never happen, however, without a concerted prayer effort.

I want to encourage you that God wants to use you in a special and unique way to see His will done right where you live. You will be able to take what you have learned in this book and not only see your personal life changed but also find your prayer niche for kingdom intercession.

Persistent Prayer for Your Nation

Before we actually get down to the nuts and bolts of how to pray specific kingdom prayers in various areas of society (government, media, etc.), let's first revisit what we studied in the last chapter concerning the *ekklesia,* or the church, and add another layer to our understanding.

Remember that I quoted Dutch Sheets, explaining that to the Romans the *ekklesia* was an assembly of people who essentially served as a congress or parliament. Then we learned that their job was to see that the culture of every conquered region was to be altered to match that of Rome.[2]

Kingdom intercession happens when the church functions

in its role as an *ekklesia* to see that, through intercessory prayer, a nation is turned back to God's will (or the biblical worldview) from the pervading culture of that particular country.

Some nations on the earth need to return, to a degree, to their covenant roots with God. This is true, in part, in my own country, the United States. Other nations may not have this kind of biblical worldview as their original foundation; in that case, a reformation is needed to bring it back to God's original intent and purpose. This will never happen in specific nations without God's people everywhere becoming involved. The Creator of the nations wants all peoples to be saved and to worship Him before His throne. I wrote *The Reformation Manifesto* because there is so much to be said about the spiritual reformation of people and nations.

Basically, we need to become God's *ekklesia* in intercessory prayer for the specific part of our nation for which we have a passion. We then need to pray for that area of society as a member of His divine *ekklesia*, legislating through our prayers for His will to be done on earth as it is in heaven.

How is that done? When we look around us, we can see that most nations are not being discipled as the Great Commission commands us to do (Matthew 28:19–20). The *ekklesia* needs to go to work, and the place to start is through informed kingdom intercession.

There are two key passages that must be understood in order *to be effective in kingdom intercession* as God's legislative body. The first has to do with binding and loosing (see chapter 9, "Proclamation Prayer"). The other is found in Isaiah 22:22.

As I mentioned in the last chapter, the terms *binding* and *loosing* were actually legal terms used by the Hebrew courts in the years Jesus walked on the earth. Either something was declared to be bound (unlawful) or loosed (legal). Another way to say this was that something either was not permitted in a society or it was permitted. Some scholars say that Matthew 18:18 could be read like this: "Whatever has already been bound in heaven, you bind on earth, and whatever has already been loosed in heaven, you loose on the earth."

These terms are used often in intercessory prayers meetings. You might hear a prayer like this: "In the name of Jesus, we bind the powers of darkness that are trying to keep abortion as the law of the land, and we loose the will of God into this area."

The other important Scripture that I mentioned, Isaiah 22:22, is also a form of binding and loosing found in the Old Testament:

> The key of the house of David I will lay upon his shoulder;
> so he shall open, and no one shall shut; and he shall shut, and
> no one shall open.

Through kingdom intercession, we become the gatekeepers of what is allowed (loosed) or forbidden (bound) in our nation. We take the keys that God took from Satan, a defeated foe at Calvary, and gave to us in order to allow or disallow certain things into our nation. We, the *ekklesia*, function as a legislative body in this manner.

Legislating in the Heavens

Years ago, intercessors in the Philippines grabbed hold of this concept of legislating in the heavens and decided to ask their weather service for the names of storms that might occur in the next year. (In the U.S., for instance, our national weather service names hurricanes [typhoons in Asia] alphabetically, alternating between male and female names.)

The Filipino prayer warriors took the list and "convened the court of heaven" in prayer. They spoke each name one by one (their list, like in the U.S., is usually made up by going through the alphabet). This is the kind of prayer they prayed that day:

"In the name of Jesus, we decree the storm *Alice* bound from our shores. We declare that you are illegal and will not enter our nation, causing destruction!"

I probably don't need to tell you this, but there were *no* violent storms that year in the Philippines. This type of kingdom intercession is a proclamation, and it goes hand in hand with the things we learned in earlier chapters about taking authority over weather patterns. We are God's legislative *ekklesia* in the earth!

The court of heaven is mentioned in more than one place in the book of Daniel. Here is one of my favorites:

> But the court shall be seated, and they shall take away his dominion, to consume and destroy it forever. Then the kingdom and dominion, and the greatness of the kingdoms under the whole heaven, shall be given to the people, the saints of the Most High, His kingdom is an everlasting kingdom, and all dominions shall serve and obey Him.
>
> DANIEL 7:26–27

Since I have learned to pray from my position in Christ in this "legislative" manner, I have had many marvelous adventures in prayer, and you can too!

The Seven-Mountain Mandate

While there are many possible ways we could become focused on kingdom prayers, it helps to use some plans already developed through two great Christian leaders: Bill Bright, the founder of

Campus Crusade for Christ, and Loren Cunningham, the founder of Youth With a Mission.

You might have heard the story of how these two men went away in 1975 to seek the Lord. During a time of prayer and fasting, God showed each of them the same spheres of society that needed to be changed in order to transform a nation: Church/Religion, Family, Government, Education, Arts/Entertainment, Media, and Business.

This insight had some traction at the time, but has become popularized in the past few years under the teaching of intercessors Lance Wallnau and Peter Wagner. Lance started calling the sectors "mountains" and coined the phrase *7M mandate*.

Now, before we begin, I want to encourage you not to be overwhelmed by this list. There is no way one person, or even one church, could effectively provide prayer covering for all of these seven areas. Instead, as you read about these seven "mountains," be sensitive to the leading of the Holy Spirit as to which one(s) He is leading you to intercede for.

We are going to take a brief look at each of these seven mountains, and read some testimonies of past and present movements, so that you can find your place in this kingdom prayer army. Remember that within each of these mountains you are the church, and you form God's *ekklesia in prayer* in that sphere of influence.

Religion

Some people call this the church mountain, but in the prayer movement we have decided to call it the religion mountain. Many people become affected by religious systems on this mountain and never try to change other sectors and spheres of influence.

It is important to note that while you may primarily be called to strengthen the local church (and this is an essential calling), we must be willing to go "into all the world" from this mountain and see nations discipled for the Lord.

It is encouraging to see that many pastors are waking up to the fact that they are responsible not only for their local congregations but also for the nation in which they live. They want to see their nation saved. Many people are drifting away from local church affiliations, and we cannot let this happen. The local church is a primary place of community, accountability, and discipleship.

If your primary calling is to this mountain, here are some suggestions on how you can be involved in kingdom intercession:

1. **Pray for your pastor.** Many people tend to criticize their pastors more than pray for them. Peter Wagner's book *Prayer Shield* is a great resource for each believer in the church.

2. **Either join or form a prayer group for in-service intercession.** In-service intercession takes place during the service itself. I have tips on how to start a prayer group in my book *Possessing the Gates of the Enemy*. What more critical hour is there in which to pray for the lost and hurting?

3. **Start a prayer group for one aspect of the church life.** One such group could be for the children's church. If your church does not have a children's intercessory group, ask if you could help spearhead one. This is a very satisfying ministry. A good resource for this is the book *Prayer-Saturated Kids* by Cheryl Sacks and Arlyn Lawrence. Here is one suggestion from their book for a prayer room right in a Sunday school classroom:

Set up a prayer closet right in your classroom—perhaps a large refrigerator box with a door and windows cut in it to give it some light, or ask a craftsman in your church to make a closet out of wood. Another possibility is to set up a quiet corner in the room separated by portable panels or curtains. Let children place in the prayer closet items such as pillows, blankets, Bibles, and Scripture verses to facilitate times of prayer. One or two children at a time may go into the prayer closet at appropriate times during the class period. They may enjoy it so much that they'll want to create a prayer closet of their own at home![3]

I believe children's prayer movements are going to sweep the nations of the world in the coming days. We need to both facilitate and teach our children to pray in corporate settings. If they learn to pray in their age-level classrooms, they will one day be able to make the leap to intergenerational prayer meetings and be a great asset to what God is doing corporately.

This leads me to one of the most important points I have made in this book: *Children are the most underutilized source of intercessory prayer in the church today.*

Many other groups in the church need prayer as well. The youth need intercession in addition to forming prayer groups in which they themselves pray.

4. **Become a prayer-saturated church.** Again, Cheryl Sacks has written an excellent and thorough book called *The Prayer-Saturated Church*, with the premise that everyone in the church should be praying—not just certain intercessory groups. This is an exciting concept, as the church is commanded to be a house of prayer for all nations. Peter Wagner's book *Churches that Pray* is an excellent resource in this area.

5. **Become a prayer missionary.** When one considers the fact that there are some 2.75 billion unreached people in

the world, the mandate for praying for the nations and people groups is clear. Nearly 41 percent of the world's population is considered to be unreached, that is, 6,650 people groups that have not been touched significantly by the gospel. We need prayer missionaries, and you don't need to leave your home to become one. A good resource for information on these unreached people groups is the Joshua Project. You can go on the Web to download prayer cards for many such people groups, one being the *Pashtun* in southern Afghanistan.

Family

If I were to name just one of the seven sectors of society that I feel the Lord is most strongly emphasizing today, it would be the family mountain. The statistics for the breakup of Christian marriages is appalling. Other research shows the number of children being pressured into having sex between the ages of ten and twelve is growing at an alarming rate. With so many problems attacking the family unit today, we need to give special attention to this mountain.

According to the Barna Group research findings, the percentage of failed marriages among born-again Christians is almost the same as among non-Christians. This should be alarming to followers of Jesus Christ—something is very, very wrong! Some Christian leaders feel that some of the marriage failures are due to a lack of teaching in the local church as well as a dearth of premarital counseling.

In the face of these findings, we cannot discount the fact that a spiritual war is waging against Christian marriages today. Here are some suggestions to help strengthen the prayer shield for this mountain:

1. **Newlywed couples prayer groups.** There is nothing like developing friendships through intercessory prayer to stand against attacks of the enemy on marriages.

2. **Prayer groups for prodigal children.** Oftentimes the heartache of prodigal children can put a heavy strain on a marriage, as Satan likes to get us to play the blame game.

3. **Find another couple that can be your prayer partners.** Why not join a covenantal fast on a particular day of the week; fast one meal for each other and/or your families.

4. **Single parents praying for and with each other.** Singles with or without children is one of the most overlooked groups in Christian circles. And single parents often feel that prayer groups—both in and out of the church—focus more on married people with families.

Don't wait for someone else to be the one to start a prayer group. If no one else is doing it, you could be the instigator. While you may not have what some might describe as a specific call to do so, there are times when the need becomes the call.

Education

This is the mountain that is probably the most important molder of minds in our societies today. If we are going to see God's kingdom come and His will done on earth, we need to see how critical our job is as intercessors for this sector.

One reason for this is because in some way we all teach someone something—either by word or example. Not only that, but part of our job description, as shown in the Great Commission, is to teach others to observe all that is commanded us in the Bible, the Creator's handbook.

Thank God for those who have "held the line" for us in prayer for our schools, such as the prayer ministry called Moms In Touch International. Fern Nichols, a praying mom, founded Moms In Touch in 1984. She is one who saw a need and filled it. Moms In Touch prayer groups are made up of two or more moms (or grandmothers) who meet regularly to pray for their children, their children's teachers, and the school administrators.

My degree from Pepperdine University is in teaching (music education), so I admit that I have a special passion to see education's sphere of influence brought into alignment with God's Word.

I include a chapter on teaching the nations in my book *The Reformation Manifesto*. And as I conducted research for that chapter, I was appalled by both the massive decline in morality on college campuses and the lack of substantive courses being taught. Not only that, but the subject matter and teaching have become more sociological in nature and biased toward humanism.

It is no wonder this has happened, given the teachings of John Dewey in the early part of the twentieth century. He is considered by many to be the father of modern education, and was one of the framers of the Humanist Manifesto, written in 1933. Here are just two points from it:

> In the place of the old attitudes involved in worship and prayer, the humanist finds his religious emotions expressed in a heightened sense of personal life and in a cooperative effort to promote social well-being. It follows that there will be no uniquely religious emotions and attitudes of the kind hitherto associated with belief in the supernatural.[4]

These statements should come as a shock to those of us in the United States who are unfamiliar with this document. Our educational system, historically, used the Word of God in its curriculum. In fact, Harvard University was described at its founding, in 1636, as the School of the Prophets. "According to a medieval tradition," explains Harvard historian Samuel Morison, "the prophet Samuel presided over the world's first university. The school received its proper name in 1638 when minister John Harvard left his entire library and a generous endowment to the young 'wilderness college' upon his death."[5]

I am tempted to write quite a bit more on this section, but there are other mountains to climb! Here are a few suggestions for prayer other than the one I gave from Moms In Touch:

1. **Pray for the school.** Form not only a prayer group but also an investigative group that researches what types of courses students are taking. Make a list of teachers and administrators and pray for them by name. Visit the school and volunteer to help when opportunities arise. This will give you a "boots on the ground" way to be both eyes and ears and to pray. Ask the local principal if you can pray on site. You might be pleasantly surprised by your principal's willingness to give permission. And of course, you can always pray while you pick up your children or drop them off at school.

2. **Pray for the school board.** Find out the names of the people on the school board, as they choose the curriculum for the classes. (At this very moment we are in a battle in my state of Texas with those who want to remove the Christian history of our nation from our textbooks.) For those of you who have read George Orwell's *1984*, describing a culture turned upside down, you can see there is

definitely something very *"Orwellian"* taking place in our schools today.[6]

3. **Form a student-led prayer group.** If you are a student, form a student-led prayer group on your campus. Thank God for the 24/7 movements that are planting houses of prayer right on campuses, as well as Sean Feucht's *Burn* worship movement. Trent Sheppard's book *God on Campus* is also an excellent resource.

   Ask for a room to form your own Prayer Club after school.

4. **Parent-directed prayer efforts.** As a parent, encourage your children to pray with other children at school. For instance, they might take a couple of minutes at lunchtime to pray for their school or teachers.

David Barton's *America: To Pray or Not to Pray* paints a vivid picture of what has happened to schools in the United States since prayer was taken out of schools in 1962. Millions of students stopped praying, and now we have kids killing other kids on our campuses. In contrast, in 1962 our biggest problem was students shooting spit-wads at each other.[7]

Government

I love the Scripture passage in Isaiah 9:6–7 that reads, "The government will be upon His shoulder. . . . [And] of the increase of His government and peace there will be no end." Since the word *kingdom* connotes a governmental structure, this mountain needs to be given massive prayer coverage. There is no sphere of influence more important than our government for which we as the *ekklesia* must "legislate in the heavens" to bring it into line with the Word of God.

Couple this with the fact that 1 Timothy 2:1–2 says that prayers and intercessions need first to be made for kings and those in authority over us so that we can lead a peaceable life. Isn't everyone interested in leading a peaceable life?

It seems to me that people are not motivated to pray for those in authority over them until there is some kind of crisis. However, we need to proactively intercede for government leaders so they will follow God's law *before* crises happen.

You may live in a country where the challenges of government are greater than other nations, and the prayer list is long and difficult. It is especially hard to pray for those with whom we do not agree; in fact, it requires great spiritual discipline to do so! Keep in mind that our heavenly Father, the King, is the great Lawgiver. He is very clear in His revealed Word that He wants His laws obeyed. However, God is not a dictator. He wants societies to choose His laws of their own volition. This is where our kingdom intercession comes into play—even in the most conflicted nations of the world.

If the gospel of the kingdom is to be preached in "all the world and then the end will come," then we have a lot of work to do before that happens. We need to pray for those in authority over us that they will come to love the Lord and want to see His laws put in place in our nations.

English Common Law, based upon the commentaries of eighteenth-century English jurist and Judge William Blackstone, is based on biblical truth. I believe the nations who follow such a system of laws (i.e., based upon God's Word) are more prosperous than other nations. It is interesting to note how a nation's prosperity declines as it turns away from making righteous decisions and laws.

I find that God will often geographically plant people in capital cities and seats of government with a special calling to intercede for their government leaders. However, we are all called to pray for those in authority over us, as is clearly stated in the Word of God. Here are some suggestions on how to accomplish this:

1. **Prayer alerts and newsletters.** Sign up for prayer alerts for ministries praying for the government. For instance, Mike and I head up a prayer ministry called *The United States Reformation Network*.[8] Currently we have a special year of prayer called *Root52,* calling the nation back to its covenantal roots with God (*52* is for the fifty-two weeks in the year). For the first two weeks, we prayed for the federal government; now we are praying for each state, one week at a time, that they might come into the union, using their state constitutions as a place to begin with a proclamation prayer. (Each of these constitutions dedicates their state to God.)

   Each week, the torch is passed in prayer through a conference call between the state prayer coordinators and their councils. We want to see each state deal with its ungodly root issues, such as freemasonry, anti-Semitism, racism, poor treatment of the native peoples, Mafia influences, occult strongholds, etc. This is a big job, as you can imagine, but the load becomes lighter when we all work and pray together. You might be the leader of a prayer network in your city or nation. If so, ask the Lord to show you a prayer strategy for your area, and use the power of kingdom intercession to see it come into line with God's plan. It is possible that your nation never had a covenant with God, and you will need to be the first generation to do so. If it was originally dedicated to God at its foundation, pray and decree that it will return to its covenantal roots.

On a recent trip to Great Britain, we had a time of prayer with the Parliamentary Prayer Group in London, and were amazed as we read the words from the Queen's coronation ceremony. These words were a profound dedication of the nation to God and of the Queen's reign under His sovereignty.

2. **Pray for your government leaders.** Make a list of the government leaders for whom God is calling you to intercede and keep it in your Bible. Call their names out to the Lord each day. Don't forget the judges of the land as well.

3. **Be informed in order to pray correctly.** Watch the news and glean from it points for your prayers, as well as subscribing to e-news services that you trust. Remember that the news of the land is the Christian's report card! It will show you the success of intercession.

4. **Join a government-focused prayer group.** Join an existing prayer group that is government-focused in nature. If you cannot find one, you might want to start one yourself. We can never have enough prayer for this important mountain!

Media

Several years ago, I flew to a number of nations and read the English language newspapers in each place. After a while I noticed a similar pattern—they were all extremely non-kingdom-of-God based. What do I mean by this? In many cases, they called evil good and good evil. They applauded things the Bible calls sinful as "advances" in civilization.

I went on a hunt after that to see if I could find one representative paper from the print media that published "the good news" while still being a secular paper. I did not find one. In fact, you could say they were propaganda machines that reported the news not even in a neutral fashion, but in a way that had an anti-biblical political spin to it.

This experience prompted me to do a similar search of the television news media. To my shock, I found much of the same. I then organized prayer teams to begin to intercede at the major news channels in New York City and other strategic locations such as Atlanta and Los Angeles. At the same time, I started receiving letters from various people who were either called to pray for this sector or were trying to survive as professionals working in the media world.

Here are some ways to pray:

1. **News reporters.** Ask God to protect those news reporters who are called to be in these influential positions.

2. **Christians in the media.** Pray that those who are representing kingdom values will come into positions of authority.

3. **Prayer for media professionals.** Form a prayer group and "adopt" various newscasters and journalists; pray that they will have an encounter with God. Don't forget local newscasters and reporters, as they influence your particular region.

4. **Christian media investment.** Intercede for Christian business leaders to have the funds to buy news channels and newspapers. Pray for favor and deep insight for those called to give the news over the Internet.

Arts and Entertainment

In some ways, the sectors of the arts and entertainment have been seen more as secular areas, set apart from the church—areas that don't involve our role as citizens of the kingdom of God. However, there is nothing that could be further from the truth.

We have largely neglected to find our roles as intercessors in these spheres of influence, and because of this we are reaping the pollution of other competing ideologies. God created creativity! That might sound unusual to you, but it's true: God is the master artist, and all creative talent and inspiration flows from Him. Unfortunately, the church has withdrawn (for the most part) from the arts and entertainment arenas. And for this reason, we have missed the opportunity to be salt and light. The result is that we are now witnessing a megalithic cultural slide that is affecting all other areas of society.

Aggressive intercession needs to take place for those who have become the "strongmen" (and women) of the arts and entertainment industries. Our friends Jonathan and Sharon Ngai live in Los Angeles, California, and operate the Reformation House of Prayer near the original site of the Azusa Street Revival. If you go into their prayer room, you will see not only prayer stations for each of the seven mountains but also pictures of various film and television personalities.

Jonathan and Sharon are aggressive in kingdom intercession. They truly believe that as they fast and pray for the influencers in the arts and entertainment industries, God will answer and bring these individuals into alignment with the destiny they were created to fulfill.

Here are some suggestions for kingdom intercession in these sectors:

1. **Missionary to the arts.** Become a prayer missionary to one aspect of either the arts or entertainment industry. Ask the Lord to show you what your portion is and toward what area you are to focus your prayers. If you are already working in this mountain, start a prayer group of your own.

2. **Pray for the influencers.** Choose those who are at the top of the mountains—those some might call the A-list—because they are going to have the greatest influence.

3. **Pray for the fine arts.** Don't forget the fine arts: ballet, dance, music, classical arts. Ask the Lord to show you how to pray. Perhaps you are a college student studying one of these mediums. Become God's prayer warrior to see each of these creative fields become holy unto the Lord.

4. **Pray for revival industry-wide.** Pray for holiness to cover the industry, whether comedy, music, dance, or drama. Ask God for a revival to sweep Hollywood, New York, Toronto, and other centers of media development.

There are a number of groups who are praying for Hollywood and the movie industry. It is exciting to see some signs of influential people being touched by Christ. I have met with people in the film industry in Asian nations and seen a move of God occurring at the highest levels.

If you live in a nation other than the United States, ask God for a prayer strategy unique to the nation in which you live. For instance, the film industry in Britain was built upon a godly foundation. Pray that it might return once again to its roots.

Business

There are many Christian leaders who have been raised up by God to focus on this mountain. Some are calling it the workplace and others the marketplace. Both my mentor Peter Wagner (*The Church in the Workplace*) and my friend Ed Silvoso (*Anointed for Business*) have greatly advanced our understanding of how God wants to work mightily through the marketplace to bring about societal and spiritual transformation.

Many prayer groups have sprung up around the world in boardrooms, and some businesses have even hired full-time intercessors to pray for and in their businesses. Mike and I have traveled with our prayer network to pray in New York City; after our time of intercession, major corruption was exposed involving leaders on Wall Street. However, there is still much work to be done in this area. Here are some suggestions:

1. **Pray with business leaders.** Start a prayer group in your local church with other business leaders. Pray for each other's businesses.

2. **Build a prayer shield.** Mobilize personal prayer partners for your business and inform them of your needs on a regular basis.

3. **Pray on the ground.** Plant prayer teams right in the financial sectors. We have heard of prayer groups meeting in and around Wall Street.

4. **Start a noontime prayer group.** Noontime prayer groups are popping up, such as the one launched by Jeremiah Lanphier after an economic crisis in 1857 in New York City. This powerful prayer meeting sparked what some have called "the businessman's revival." Churches across the city were filled with people praying, and some

businesses changed their lunch hour from 11:55 to 1:05 to accommodate the pray-ers. My friends Hal and Cheryl Sacks, of Bridgebuilders International in Phoenix, Arizona, have started a noontime prayer meeting and it is gaining momentum. I believe there will be another sweeping revival among businesspeople stirred up by noontime prayers as in Lanphier's time.

It is critical to apply all that we have learned about persistent prayer if we are ever to see these seven mountains of society aligned with God's plan for them. The battle cry for this move of kingdom prayer and intercession will shake everything that can be shaken, all that is not aligned with God's will. We will see awakenings and these mountains of society reformed and transformed if we persist in prayer. All things are possible with God—even the restoration of biblical values. And it is possible to disciple and teach others the things of the Lord, or Jesus would never have commissioned us to such a task!

Don't become fainthearted in the battle for the part God calls you to as we pray together: *Let your kingdom come and your will be done on earth as it is in heaven.*

Conclusion

*P*ersistent, sustained prayer can be difficult. But I am convinced there are many seemingly unanswered prayers because we give up too soon. As our time together ends, reflect on your own unanswered prayers. Are there prayers you used to pray that you no longer voice? Was it for a loved one to be saved? How about your finances?

Take a few moments and reflect on each chapter of this book. Use the material as a life manual, and check from time to time to see if you have had failures in certain areas of your prayer life.

Let's recap:

1. RECORD IN YOUR BIBLE WHAT YOU PRAYED, FOR WHOM YOU PRAYED, AND THE DATE

If you are comfortable writing in your Bible, jot down the date and make a note beside the Scripture that pertains to a specific promise of God that you want to see fulfilled. This will serve to encourage you for years to come. Just this morning, I opened my Bible and saw a promise I had claimed in 1987, and remembered how the Lord had marvelously answered that prayer for a miracle.

2. KEEP YOUR OWN PRAYER JOURNAL

You also might want to keep a journal of what you prayed and for whom, and then go back over it and record the date that God answered your prayers. Write a note of thanksgiving to God for what He has done. These precious missives and notations can be left for your family generations and for those you are mentoring. Peter Wagner says that any move of God that isn't written down gets lost in the generations. We don't want our prayer victories to be lost to others because we didn't record them! We can provide solace and grace to both ourselves and those after us who might read our journal.

3. BE AN ENCOURAGER

After you learn these secrets to answered prayer, take time to sit down with a group of friends over coffee to discuss the points with them. Don't wait for someone else to be the encourager. Be the one to begin. There is nothing like a prayer group to stand with you and encourage you in your darkest nights and most difficult situations.

Start to pray, and soon you will have your own secrets of prayer to share with others.

Never underestimate the power of persistent prayer!

—Cindy

Questions for Individual and Group Study

Chapter One: *Why Pray?*

1. Have you ever wondered why we need to pray when God already knows everything about us?
2. Do you believe you need to ask God for even your basic needs?
3. Does God want you to talk with Him about everything in your life? Does He care?
4. Should our prayers include praying for our cities and nations?
5. Explain why we need to pray and ask God for answers.

Chapter Two: *The Case for Persistent Prayer*

1. Why do we need to pray more than once for a particular prayer request?

2. Are there times when it seems to you that your prayers are not answered?

3. Do you ever get tired of being persistent in your prayer life?

4. How can you encourage others to be persistent in their prayers until they see them answered?

5. Do you have a testimony from being persistent in your prayers for a certain person or situation? Either write about it or share it with another person.

Chapter Three: *Praying the Will of God*

1. Can you ever really know the will of God for your life?

2. Do you feel confident that God hears you when you pray? If not, why?

3. How did George Müller become so certain that God would answer his prayers?

4. Do you mistrust God in any way? If so, when did it begin? Ask God to restore you to a place of trusting Him.

5. Make a list of things that need to change in your life and pray with authority over them each day.

Chapter Four: *Blockages to Answered Prayer*

1. Have you ever suffered a trauma that "shipwrecked" you in your faith?

2. If so, ask the Holy Spirit to heal your hurt. Confess your pain to Him and ask God to restore you.

3. Do you have areas of unforgiveness in your life that are hindering your prayers? Take time alone with God to confess any unforgiveness you are harboring in your heart.

4. Bitterness can sometimes be hidden behind self-justification. Continue on your journey to answered prayer by

asking God to shine His light of revelation on pockets of bitterness in your life.

5. Have you developed areas of unbelief in your life through disappointments? Recognize them and ask God to forgive you and restore your faith in Him.

Chapter Five: *Fasting*

1. Have you ever fasted? If so, share your experience with another person.

2. What are some benefits of fasting?

3. How do you prepare for a fast? What should you do to end a fast?

4. What happened when Daniel fasted twenty-one days? How were his prayers answered?

5. Have you ever fasted about a cause such as to see abortion end in your country or for human trafficking to be exposed?

Chapter Six: *Praying the Word*

1. Start a prayer journal. You can either buy a paper one or use an electronic version. You might want to purchase a Bible for writing in and underlining as your journal. Some people use different colored highlighters for different kinds of promises. Others might want to purchase a book such as *Prayers that Avail Much* by Germaine Copeland to use for study and encouragement.

2. Why is it a good idea to use Scripture when we pray? How does it increase our authority in intercession?

3. Share with another person or journal about a favorite verse that you have used in your prayer life.

4. Choose the most challenging situation you are presently

facing and write out a Scripture-based prayer for times of intercession.

5. Make a list of elected officials in your city and nation. Talk about recent news in your city or nation and how Scripture praying can facilitate the placement of righteous leaders. Pray in concert with others for these local and national officials (1 Timothy 2:1–2).

Chapter Seven: *Persistent Praise*

1. Dialogue about the ways that praise can be considered prayer and vice versa.

2. Name a time when you witnessed a spiritual breakthrough through praising God.

3. Have you ever chosen to praise God in the midst of a difficult circumstance? Tell about the results in your group or journal about it.

4. Give Dick Eastman's definition of intercessory worship and describe the power of praise in world missions.

5. Choose a nation for which you will be a prayer missionary. You might get a map and ask the Lord to direct you to a specific nation. Praying for an unreached people group is a good way to start. For information on those who need prayer, you can also go to the Web site of the Joshua Project.

Chapter Eight: *Intergenerational Prayer*

1. Is lineage important to God?

2. Are you developing your own spiritual legacy?

3. Do you ever pray with someone in another generation other than your own? Tell or write a testimony about your experience.

4. What are some ways that families can develop prayer times together? If you do not have Christian family members to pray with you, find someone who will become your family in Christ and pray with them.

5. What are some ways to facilitate intergenerational prayer?

Chapter Nine: *Proclamation Prayer*

1. What is proclamation prayer?

2. Have you ever prayed for a change in weather and seen an answer?

3. How does one know when a proclamation prayer is in order to see God's kingdom come and His will done on earth as it is in heaven?

4. Define the meaning of the *ekklesia*. What is its role on the earth?

5. What actually transpires when we "bind" and "loose" in intercessory proclamations?

Chapter Ten: *Kingdom Intercession*

1. Define kingdom intercession.

2. Name a way in which you have prayed for the kingdom of God to advance in your life, in your city, or in your nation.

3. Name the seven mountains of society.

4. With which of the seven mountains do you most identify? Discuss why this is true.

5. Are there certain mountains of society that all believers need to focus on regardless of their own personal calling or interest?

Acknowledgments

Writing a book has its unique set of challenges, and includes moments of both joy and despair. The creative process rarely includes just the author, but many others whom the process affects. For this reason, acknowledgments not only show our gratitude to others who have had a part, but in some fashion make it up to the people who were in the "fellowship of suffering" during the whole season we call *writing a book*. One can only laugh about some things afterward, as most of us groan our way through the effort (with the exception of author geniuses like Peter Wagner, who put us all to shame). We love the end result, but don't like the pressure that comes with putting our inspiration down "on paper."

First of all, thank you, Jesus, for helping me finish this book in the midst of an intense travel schedule!

Second only to Jesus, I would like to deeply thank my husband,

Mike. I find that he sincerely loves me and doesn't like sharing me with a computer. He tolerates it because he also likes the end result, but I frankly owe him a vacation in Maui. Thanks, Michael, my sweetheart of thirty-seven years. I'll make it up to you on the sandy beaches of Hawaii—I promise! Also, thanks to the rest of the Jacobs clan.

Also, Elizabeth Tiam-Fook, my assistant, who gave extra hours after work to make readable what I am sending off to my editor, Kyle Duncan. Elizabeth, I am deeply grateful. Kyle, what can I say? You are simply the best editor and friend. Not only that, but you have put up with me through five books. Now that is the power of persistent prayer!

I could not forget the wonderful staff at Generals International as well. They have prayed me through and supported me. Also thanks to my little sister, Lucy Reithmiller, and Cheryl Sacks (two of my lifelong prayer partners); my mother, Eleanor Lindsay, and her husband, Thomas; the GI prayer partners; and my pastors, Jim and Becky Hennesy.

 Notes

CHAPTER ONE

1. *Spirit-Filled Life Bible* (Nashville: Thomas Nelson, 1991), 5.

2. Paul E. Billheimer, *Destined for the Throne* (Fort Washington, PA: Christian Literature Crusade, 1975), 15.

3. Dutch Sheets, *Intercessory Prayer* (Ventura, CA: Regal Books, 1996), 32.

4. James Strong, *Strong's Exhaustive Concordance of the Bible* (Grand Rapids, MI: Zondervan), 154.

CHAPTER TWO

1. *http://www.sermonnotebook.org/ The Power of Persistent Prayer*, 2.

2. Ibid., 2.

3. J. Kirk Johnston, *Why Christians Sin* (Grand Rapids, MI: Discovery House, 1992), 39–41. *www.christianglobe.com.* Story has been paraphrased.

4. *http://www.sermonnotebook.org*

5. Cindy Jacobs, *Possessing the Gates of the Enemy* (Grand Rapids, MI: Chosen Books, 2009), 50–51.

CHAPTER 3

1. P. L. Tan, (1996, c.1979), *Encyclopedia of 7700 Illustrations* (Garland, TX: Bible Communications), Illustration 1494: "Got to Be in Quebec."

2. *Dictionary.com*

3. *Note:* Some Texans still wear cowboy hats, boots, and belts to this day, to the surprise of many of our international guests who come to Dallas for a visit.

4. Jacobs, *Possessing the Gates of the Enemy,* 3rd edition, 45.

5. W. C. Kaiser, *Hard Sayings of the Bible* (Downers Grove, IL: InterVarsity, 1996), 740.

6. The Hebrew word is *Nathan; Strong's Exhaustive Concordance of the Bible.*

7. Dutch Sheets, *Authority in Prayer* (Minneapolis: Bethany House, 2006), 42.

8. For those of you who are not aware, the name of our worldwide television ministry is *GodKnows.tv*.

CHAPTER 4

1. Dick Eastman, *Dick Eastman on Prayer* (Fort Washington, PA: Global Christian Publishers, 1999), 43.

2. Ibid., 41.

3. Ethelbert W. Bullinger, *A Critical Lexicon and Concordance to the English and Greek New Testament* (Grand Rapids, MI: Zondervan, 1975), 400.

4. Dutch Sheets, *Intercessory Prayer,* 138–139.

5. *Dick Eastman on Prayer,* 108–109.

CHAPTER 5

1. Arthur Wallis, *God's Chosen Fast* (Fort Washington, PA: Christian Literature Crusade, 1968), 82–83.

2. Holy Club, *http://en.wikipedia.org/wiki/Holy-Club*

3. Bob Rodgers, *101 Reasons to Fast* (Louisville, KY: Bob Rodgers Ministries, 1995).

4. Wallis, *God's Chosen Fast,* 98.

5. Bob Rodgers, *The Hundred-Fold Blessing* (Louisville, KY: Bob Rodgers Ministries, 2007), 18.

6. Derek Prince, *Shaping History Through Prayer and Fasting* (New Kensington, PA: Whitaker House, 1973, 2002), Introduction.

7. Rodgers, *101 Reasons to Fast,* 9.

CHAPTER 6

1. Germaine Copeland, *Prayers That Avail Much,* 25th Anniversary Edition (Tulsa, OK: Harrison House, 1997), 345–357.

2. Written and compiled using the 1863 Proclamation of Abraham Lincoln, calling for a National Day of Prayer and Fasting.

3. E. M. Bounds, *E. M. Bounds on Prayer* (New Kensington, PA: Whitaker House, 1997), 246.

CHAPTER 7

1. Jacobs, *Possessing the Gates of the Enemy,* 3rd edition, 165.

2. Tommy Walker, *Songs from Heaven with Phil Kassel* (Ventura, CA: Regal Books, 2005), 20.

3. Chuck Pierce and John Dickson, *The Worship Warrior* (Ventura, CA: Regal Books, 2002), 58.

4. Dick Eastman, *Heights of Delight* (Ventura, CA: Regal Books, 2002), 24–26.

CHAPTER 8

1. Taken from the "Word Wealth" section of the *Spirit-Filled Life Bible*, 22.

2. Eastman, *Pathways of Delight* (Ventura, CA: Regal Books, 2002), 70, 72, 74, 78.

3. Quin Sherrer, *Prayers from a Grandma's Heart* (Grand Rapids, MI: Inspiro, the Gift Group of Zondervan, 2001), 16.

4. Edward K. Rowell, *Fresh Illustrations for Preaching and Teaching* (Grand Rapids, MI: Baker, 1997), 165.

5. Cheryl Sacks and Arlyn Lawrence, *Prayer-Saturated Kids* (Colorado Springs: NavPress, 2007), 140.

CHAPTER 9

1. Bill Johnson, *www.bethel.org,* "Tijuana Revolution" (March 2005).

2. Sheets, *Authority in Prayer,* 61.

3. Cindy Jacobs, *Deliver Us from Evil* (Ventura, CA: Regal Books, 2001), 34.

4. Ibid., 35.

5. Paraphrased from Gary Kinnaman, *Overcoming the Dominion of Darkness* (Tarrytown, NY: Chosen Books, 1990), 54, 56–58.

6. General editor, Jack Hayford, *Spirit-Filled Life Bible* (Nashville: Thomas Nelson, 1991), 1419.

7. Sheets, *Authority in Prayer,* 59.

8. Dick Eastman, *The Purple Pig and Other Miracles* (Monroeville, PA: Whitaker House, 1974), 84–87.

CHAPTER 10

1. Cindy Jacobs, *The Reformation Manifesto* (Minneapolis: Bethany House, 2008), 33–34. (Quote taken from Darrow Miller's *Discipling Nations,* 139.)

2. Sheets, *Authority in Prayer,* 61.

3. Sacks and Lawrence, *Prayer-Saturated Kids,* 121.

4. Jacobs, *The Reformation Manifesto,* 115.

5. Trent Sheppard, *God on Campus* (Downers Grove, IL: InterVarsity Press, 2009), 32.

6. *Note:* For more on this subject, I suggest you read Jim Nelson Black's *Freefall of the American University,* which gives stunning examples of this kind of Orwellian change that is happening on our campuses. He also gives startling information on formerly godly universities such as Harvard.

7. For those not familiar with this American childhood pastime, a spit-wad is made by wetting the paper wrapping of a drinking straw and then shooting it at someone by blowing through the straw, or simply wetting a small wad of paper and blowing it through the straw.

8. You can sign up to receive prayer alerts from The United States Reformation Network on our Web site, *www.generals.org.*

Subject Index